DATE DUE

DEMCO 38-296

Jon'a F. Meyer

Inaccuracies
in Children's Testimony
Memory, Suggestibility,
or Obedience to Authority?

Pre-publication
REVIEWS,
COMMENTARIES,
EVALUATIONS . . .

"**J**on'a F. Meyer illuminates the most critical and difficult aspect of prosecuting crimes against children, i.e., the believability of the child victim/witness. This book is a must read for attorneys, investigators, and victim advocates regarding the use of child testimony in cases involving the abuse and exploitation of children. No prosecutor's, investigator's, or child advocate's library will be complete without this book."

Stanley V. Pennington, JD
Assistant Professor,
Department of Criminology,
Indiana State University

"**C**ourts should never doubt children's testimony, especially when it comes to sexual abuse cases. How could a child describe what he or she doesn't know?

This book provides a lucid, carefully researched, and well-written answer to this question. In sum, children do seem to be affected by authority, especially when asked leading questions. Therefore, Dr. Meyer outlines the steps necessary to ensure accurate testimony from children. These steps make this book a 'must read' for those who study or work directly with children's testimony."

Tara Gray, PhD
Assistant Professor,
Department of Criminal Justice,
New Mexico State University

More pre-publication
REVIEWS, COMMENTARIES, EVALUATIONS . . .

"**T**his is an exceptional book because it is applicable to the multiple disciplines and variety of academic participants (educators/students/researchers) as well as establishments in the community-at-large that must make judgments based on testimonial information. Dr. Meyer's unbiased presentation of research methods plus conclusions through historical times about the validity of children's testimonies leaves the reader with knowledge and insights into child behavior and adult responses. Even though the title of the text accurately portrays the contents, there is an additional included benefit: that of inaccuracies of adults as they can falter in memory, be victimized by suggestibility, and have obedience to their selected authority figures—just as children experience!

I have already recommended this book to colleagues in legal anthropology, police science, criminal justice, psychology, sociology, philosophy, early childhood development, members of the ABA and CBA, parole officers, child care centers, marriage and family counselors, pastors, principals of elementary and secondary schools, pediatric nurses, and a playwright."

Gloria J. Bogdan, PhD
Professor of Anthropology,
Orange Coast College,
Costa Mesa, CA

"**T**his book provides a comprehensive view of the classical and contemporary literature on obedience to authority and suggestibility. The author takes a distinctive approach by combining the two bodies of literature and applying them to a pressing problem in today's litigious society—children testifying in court. The author selects well-publicized cases to illustrate the pitfalls of children as witnesses. Application of classical research on obedience to authority and suggestibility to this contemporary problem promotes insight into the validity of testimony. The effects of stress, prompting, and imagination on recall are also addressed. The author presents plausible remedies to increase the accuracy of children's testimony and recall, as well as suggestions for future research. The use of actual testimony from interesting cases, in conjunction with a clear writing style, creates a highly readable and useful book."

Deborah A. Parsons, PhD
Assistant Professor,
Department of Criminal Justice,
California State University,
San Bernadino

Inaccuracies in Children's Testimony

Memory, Suggestibility, or Obedience to Authority?

HAWORTH Criminal Justice,
Forensic Behavioral Sciences,
& Offender Rehabilitation
Nathaniel J. Pallone, PhD
Senior Editor

New, Recent, and Forthcoming Titles:

Treating Sex Offenders in Correctional Institutions and Outpatient Clinics: A Guide to Clinical Practice by William E. Prendergast

The Merry-Go-Round of Sexual Abuse: Identifying and Treating Survivors by William E. Prendergast

Chaplains to the Imprisoned: Sharing Life with the Incarcerated by Richard Denis Shaw

Forensic Neuropsychology: Conceptual Foundations and Clinical Practice by José A. Valciukas

Inaccuracies in Children's Testimony: Memory, Suggestibility, or Obedience to Authority? by Jon'a F. Meyer

Inaccuracies in Children's Testimony
Memory, Suggestibility, or Obedience to Authority?

Jon'a F. Meyer

The Haworth Press
New York • London

The Haworth Press, Inc., 10 Alice Street, Binghamton, NY 13904-1580

Library of Congress Cataloging-in-Publication Data

Meyer, Jon'a, 1967–
  Inaccuracies in children's testimony : memory, suggestibility, or obedience to authority? / Jon'a F. Meyer.
      p.   cm.
  Includes bibliographical references and index.
  ISBN 0-7890-0167-5 (alk. paper)
  1. Child witnesses. 2. Memory in children. 3. Recollection (Psychology). I. Title.
K2271.5.Z9M49 1997
347'.066'083–dc21
                                                                                    96-51807
                                                                                    CIP

For my parents, Jon and Faye,
and for Paul Jesilow

Malama pono, Malama i na kupuna
Be righteous and cherish the heritage of our ancestors

ABOUT THE AUTHOR

Jon'a Forestine Meyer, PhD, is Assistant Professor in the Department of Sociology at Rutgers University in Camden. She is the author of many professional articles and book chapters on topics such as bias in judicial sentencing, prison reform, child witnesses in abuse cases, and public attitudes toward the police. Her research has been supported by grants from the National Institute of Justice, the National Institute of Mental Health, and the American Sociological Association. She has participated in many conferences and workshops and has been an invited speaker to present her work and expertise on issues such as criminology and anthropology, technology in criminal justice, drunk drivers in the courts, crime seriousness ratings, and children's obedience to authority. Dr. Meyer is a member of the American Sociological Association, the Association of American Indian and Alaska Native Professors, the American Society of Criminology, and the Academy of Criminal Justice Science.

CONTENTS

Preface

This book combines the literatures on obedience to authority with those on suggestibility to create a third literature. These first two literatures, although discussed separately in academic works, are related. A study of children's responses to obedience is presented to shed further light on a possible cause of suggestibility, defined here as the alteration of reports from a correct recollection about an event as a consequence of postevent information regarding the incident. Suggestions for future research are presented at the conclusion of the book.

How children are questioned to learn what they have witnessed is crucial due to the effects the questioning sessions may have on their testimony. This book examines children's testimony from several perspectives and suggests how we may increase children's abilities to testify accurately. The first chapter discusses children's memory in the courtroom and what they are able to remember. Chapter 2 reviews the literature on the effects of stress, prompting, and imagination on children's recall. The third chapter presents information on suggestibility in adults and children. The fourth chapter examines realities in the research on children's suggestibility, including sources of suggestibility. The fifth chapter reviews the research on obedience to authority and discusses how it can explain children's behavior as witnesses. The sixth chapter discusses Milgram's theory of obedience to authority in some detail, tying it to children as witnesses. The final chapter suggests ways to increase the accuracy of children's recall, and introduces ideas for future research.

Acknowledgments

I express my deepest appreciation to my doctoral advisor, Paul Jesilow, who has been a source of inspiration, support, and friendship. His guidance and patience helped make this book possible. I will always remember and honor him in all I do.

I thank Gilbert Geis and Richard McCleary for their comments on earlier versions, which helped strengthen my arguments and prose. I also thank Gabriela Buchenau and Renee Laroche for their generous assistance in translating the German and French sources discussed in this book.

I also thank the many instructors who have instilled in me a desire to find answers through research. In particular, I thank Joe Charles Bond, Harold Charnofsky, Karen Pugh Lakin, and Herman Loether. Their guidance and influence have made a difference in my life. I also thank Kenneth Chew and Cassia Spohn, who mentored me and encouraged me to achieve my goals.

Lastly, I thank my friends and family. My father gave of himself his knowledge about life and his insatiable desire to learn. My mother gave me the ambition to fulfill my personal goals and the need to respect the others with whom I share this place. My friends were tremendous sources of happiness and supported me when times were difficult. I thank them all, but foremost among them are Gloria and Tom Bogdan, Judy Case, Jody Crowley, Diana Grant, Tara Gray, Paul Jesilow, Deborah Parsons, and Sanjeev Sridharan. To Richard Paul and Jaime Chavez, I simply say, "Stay safe."

Chapter 1

Children's Memory in the Courtroom: What Do Children Remember?

Generally, children's honesty is only of concern to their parents, teachers, or others who have authority over them. Occasionally, however, the state becomes interested in the accuracy of children's statements, especially when they provide testimony in legal cases. This book reviews research that explores whether children may give false testimony when provided with leading questions. It argues that an overlooked literature in the study of children's testimony may be research on obedience to authority and that adding this perspective may provide researchers with a new paradigm through which to view and understand children's behavior when they testify or provide other legally relevant statements.

IDENTIFYING A SOCIAL PROBLEM

The current anxiety about the validity of children's testimony in courts stems from heavily publicized cases of child molestation during the 1980s. By far the most widely known incident was the McMartin Preschool case in Manhattan Beach, California.[1] The owners of the school, Raymond Buckey and his mother, Virginia McMartin, and five former teachers were charged with 208 counts of child molestation and conspiracy after the police were inundated with a sea of complaints that began when a two-year-old sodomy victim named Raymond Buckey as his assailant. The nation was shocked as the story, covered daily in the media, began to unfold into one of the most heinous crimes of the time. Some children told of forced participation in "naked games," fondling, penetration, photography sessions, and ritualistic behavior, including animal sacrifices to frighten the young victims into silence about the clandestine activities in which they were key participants.

The defense argued that the young victim-witnesses had been coached into testifying as they did about the incidents. They further alleged that the children were questioned in a suggestive manner that led them to invent the false charges of abuse: "We believe that perhaps a method . . . used in questioning these children and in having them discuss what occurred and who was involved (may have resulted in) preconditioning these children" (*Los Angeles Times*, April 21, 1984). To bolster their theory, the defense questioned the first young witness, a seven-year-old boy, who admitted during trial that he had testified as he did to please some of the adults involved in the prosecution of the case (*Los Angeles Times*, January 25, 1985):

Defense: "They told you they wanted you to say that Ray [key defendant Raymond Buckey] touched the kids on the penis and the butt?"
Child: "Yes."

. . .

Defense: [Did you say Virginia McMartin watched the molestations] "so that he [Deputy District Attorney Glenn Stevens] wouldn't be sad?"
Child: "Yes."

. . .

Defense: "This is just telling the story these people want you to tell? You're not nervous, but just telling the story that Shawn [Shawn Connerly, a therapist who questioned the child], Mr. Stevens [the prosecutor], and your mom—that everybody—wants you to tell?"
Child: "Yes."

Indeed, the original questioning of the children was full of legal difficulties. Often, the interviewers coaxed the children into telling "yucky secrets." Interviewing techniques employed by social workers may be therapeutic in nature, that is focusing on helping the child deal with the trauma of abuse. The Vermont Sexual Abuse/ Assault Protocol for investigating possible incidents of abuse of children and adolescents states: "While the primary goal of both is to protect the child, the police officer remains concerned with the investigation of criminal activity; the Social and Rehabilitative Services worker with such issues as family dynamics and treatment" (Young 1988, p. 255). Ann Burgess and her associates (Burgess, Holmstrom, and McCausland 1978, p. 183) state:

> The most important technique [when counseling young victims of sexual traumas] is to encourage the child to talk about the incident. If the child does not bring the subject up in discussion, the counselor should tell the child it is important to discuss it. . . . If the child talks, the counselor encourages discussion.

This fundamental distinction certainly dealt the prosecutors in the McMartin case a traumatic blow. When a lack of evidence to corroborate the children's sometimes fanciful accounts was coupled with the controversial techniques used in questioning the young witnesses, charges were dropped against five of the defendants, leaving only Raymond Buckey and his mother to stand trial. In the end, a chagrined Los Angeles District Attorney Ira Reiner concluded: "The evidence against the others is weak" (*Los Angeles Times*, January 18, 1986).

After the longest and costliest trial in U.S. history, both defendants were acquitted on all but fourteen of the charges and the jury deadlocked on these remaining charges (twelve sex-abuse charges against Raymond Buckey and a conspiracy count against both Raymond Buckey and his mother). The conspiracy charges were dropped before a new hearing date was set for the remaining counts against Raymond Buckey.

The jurors based their inability to convict either defendant on their belief that the interviewers had led the children to their stories. One juror summed up this concern with the questioning process: "The interviewers at Children's Institute International [where the children were interviewed] asked questions in such a leading manner that we never got the children's stories in their own words" (*Orange County Register*, January 19, 1990). The case was essentially lost, then, before the charges were even filed due to the way the child victims were asked about their experiences.

The later trial of Raymond Buckey on the remaining counts resulted in a hung jury; the district attorney chose not to proceed further with the case (*Los Angeles Times*, July 28, 1990). Thus ended the infamous McMartin trial. Future prosecutors now know the lesson learned by District Attorney Ira Reiner: pay particular attention to how accounts are obtained from young witnesses.

The Wee Care Day Nursery case in Maplewood, New Jersey, also focused attention on the questioning of children. In May, 1985, an investigation was launched into the possibility that one of the nursery's teachers, Kelly Michaels, molested a number of her students. Several factors in the case, which were disclosed during the heat of the McMartin preliminary hearing, worked to the prosecution's benefit: the discovery of some corroborating evidence, including an unusual poem written by Michaels in her grade book; the ability of the children to validate each other's testimony through seemingly consistent reports; and the careful video recording of many interviews with the child witnesses.

As in the McMartin case, the methods used in questioning the child witnesses came under fire by the defense in an attempt to get the 235-count indictment involving thirty-one children against their client dismissed. The methods used to interview the children possessed elements present in the McMartin case (which, at the time of the Wee Care investigation, still seemed very strong for the prosecution[2]). In her book on the Wee Care case, Lisa Manshel (1990, pp. 55-56, 80) presents several exchanges between child and interviewer that demonstrate some of the methods used to question the children.

> *Interviewer:*   "Okay, . . . I hear that you want to help me investigate and crack this case wide open. Come on, you were so brave last time."
>
>   . . .
>
> *Interviewer:*   "How did it feel when she hit you on the penis? I can't hear ya, buddy."
> *Boy, age five:*   "Bad."
> *Interviewer:*   "You feel better now that you started talking, it's not a big secret anymore?"

Boy, age five: "Yeah."
Interviewer: "We talked to a few more of your buddies. We
                    talked to everybody now . . . And everyone told
                    me about the nap room stuff and the bathroom
                    stuff and the music room stuff and the peanut
                    butter stuff and the pee stuff and everything. So
                    nothing surprises me anymore."
                              . . .

Boy, age four: "I hate you."
Interviewer: "No you don't
Boy, age four: "Yes I do."
Interviewer: "No you don't
Boy, age four: "Yes I do."
Interviewer: "You just don't like talking about this, but you
                    don't hate me. Did Kelly [the defendant] ever tell
                    you that she could turn you into a mouse?"
Boy, age four: "Yeah."
Interviewer: "She did . . .?"
Boy, age four: "Yeah."
Interviewer: "And what did she say she would turn into?"
Boy, age four: "A monster."
Interviewer: "Did she say she would turn you into a . . .
                    monster?"
Boy, age four: "Yeah."
Interviewer: "You didn't believe that stuff, did you?"
Boy, age four: "No."
Interviewer: "But it scared you a little bit?"
Boy, age four: "Yep."
Interviewer: "Yeah, it scared me too.
Boy, age four: "Bluh, I'm big. Ha ha, I'm almost five."
Interviewer: "When are you gonna be five? When's your
                    birthday?"
Boy, age four: "In the fall."
Interviewer: "In the fall? Oh come on, you gonna help us out?"
Boy, age four: "Yeah."
Interviewer: "Do you want to help us keep her in jail longer?
                    Huh? Do ya, huh?"

Boy, age four: "Uh, ooh."
Interviewer: "Do you want to help us keep her in jail longer?"

Ultimately, the judge hearing the case did not agree with the defense's argument: "I see no overreaching by the State . . . no evidence that individual testimony was tainted. . . . The children were not brainwashed or forced to do anything. . . . There is absolutely no reason to dismiss any of the counts in this indictment on the grounds sought by the defense" (Manshel 1990, p. 125). The jury also failed to find the questioning techniques so tainting that they prevented accurate testimony, and Michaels was convicted.

The conviction was appealed to the New Jersey Supreme Court, however, based on the defense's concerns regarding the manner in which the children were interviewed. In a unanimous verdict, the state's highest court reversed the convictions and ordered the trial court to hold a pretrial taint hearing to assess the reliability of each child's testimony before allowing him/her to testify in court (*State v. Michaels.* [1994]. 136 N.J. 299; 642 A.2d 1372). The court took issue with the manner in which the interviews were conducted, arguing that the prosecutors and investigators substantially shaped the children's accounts:

> In conclusion, we find that the interrogations that occurred in this case were improper and there is a substantial likelihood that the evidence derived from them is unreliable. (*State v. Michaels* 1994, p. 50)

At that point, the prosecution dropped all charges against Michaels (Ceci and Bruck 1995, p. 13). In addition to the Wee Care case, a number of other cases involving children as witnesses are discussed and analyzed in detail by Stephen Ceci and Maggie Bruck in their 1995 monograph, to which the interested reader is referred for additional material.

QUESTIONING OF CHILDREN

Because of cases such as Wee Care and McMartin, the methods used to question children have changed. Inger Sagatun and Leonard

Edwards (1988, p. 3) report that child witnesses were once sub-jected to being interviewed twenty or more times by individuals from different agencies seeking the same information. Now, authorities try to see that sessions are videotaped to spare the child additional interviews. These videotapes can then be viewed by numerous individuals on different occasions without the necessity of asking the child what happened each time, thereby reducing the trauma to the child and chances of the child changing his or her testimony to fit each interviewer's mode of questioning.

The State of California Guidelines for the Investigation of Child Physical Abuse and Neglect, Child Sexual Abuse and Exploitation (The Commission on Peace Officer Standards and Training, 1986, guideline number 59) specifically address minimizing the number of interviews conducted with child victim-witnesses. The guidelines suggest working with other agencies that may be interested in the child's accounts and conducting thorough interviews, as well as the use of audio and/or video recording of the interviews. The Guidelines (1986, guideline number 62) recommend three important precautions: (1) allow the child to describe the incident in his or her own words; (2) avoid influencing the child's account of the alleged offense; and (3) avoid being judgmental when discussing the alleged suspect. Guidelines such as these reflect a formalized move to avoid influences on the child witness' account by interviewers.

CHILDREN'S TESTIMONY

The issue of children's veracity is not new to the courtroom. There were cases in Puritan times in which youngsters' testimony was responsible for the imprisonment and execution of a number of individuals accused of being witches. Salem Village, Massachusetts, was ensured a permanent place in history when in 1692, a group of girls seemingly afflicted with twitching fits and lack of concentration, among other maladies, were diagnosed by the local physician as having "an evil hand upon them" (Starkey 1949, p. 23). The community of Salem Village became fanatical in a search for the "evil hand," and began to press the girls to name their afflictors:

When the ministers asked them to name who afflicted them, they drew a blank. The girls fell dumb. No one had afflicted them; it had just happened.

> Their impotence dismayed their guardians. Witchcraft was afoot and could not for the safety of the commonwealth be allowed to go unchecked. But the witches could not be identified without the help of the girls. . . . The girls must somehow be made to pull themselves together and concentrate on the problem; certainly God in His mercy would give them power to name their tormentors. (Starkey 1949, p. 29)

It is important to note that the authorities needed the girls' help in identifying the witches. Adults at the time not only earnestly believed in the presence of witchcraft, but also felt that children were best able to distinguish witches because their "innocence" allowed them see certain "evils" that adults could not (Ceci, Toglia, and Ross 1990, p. 289). Therefore, children became key witnesses in witchcraft proceedings: "Adults not only *could* accept a child's testimony in this regard, they *had* to accept it because their lost innocence compromised their own ability to recognize evil" (Ceci, Toglia, and Ross 1990, p. 289). This also meant, however, that the girls' accounts could not be questioned by adults.

One by one, local villagers of all walks of life were decried as witches by the girls, tried, and executed.[3] The entire incident is now looked upon with great scorn and contempt, since the passage of time has shown that no devils were loosed in Massachusetts, contrary to what the girls testified to in 1692. It is still unknown whether the girls deliberately lied about the accusations, or if they "were truly convinced of the accuracy of their testimony" (Ceci, Toglia, and Ross 1990, p. 286).[4]

The Salem witch trials and child sexual abuse allegations have more in common than the presence of testimony by children. Gilbert Geis and Ivan Bunn (1991, p. 40) draw other parallels between the two phenomena:

> How do you satisfactorily rebut the claim that you were seen flying over rooftops last night, and that the person in your bed

during that period was a diabolic substitute? Or, for that matter, that you privately sexually abused a child?

Geis and Bunn (1991) warn against lessening the protections currently offered to defendants, cautioning that the urge to protect children from potential abusers should not be allowed to overcome the need for adequate protections for those accused of the offense: "Given the lesson of the witchcraft period, it seems wise to be notably vigilant about the legitimacy of complaints of child sexual abuse" (p. 41).

LEGAL HISTORY

Children's testimony has been a concern throughout most of legal history. Under common law, children were not allowed to testify prior to the age of seven years. The courts argued that such young witnesses were unable to understand the oaths involved with testifying (Goodman 1984a, p. 12). Between the ages of seven and fourteen, children might be determined competent to provide testimony. Tests sought to determine if the child understood the oath of truth or believed in the necessity of truth for moral reasons (Goodman 1984a, pp. 12-13).

Competency to testify is normally assumed to be fourteen years of age in the United States, requiring children thirteen years of age and younger to submit to questioning by a judge to determine their ability to accurately understand, recall, and report on the events under question, "with this inquiry being more searching in proportion to the child's immaturity (Marin et al. 1979, p. 296).

The testimony of children has become of intense interest to the legal community as more and more cases involving children, both as victims and witnesses, are brought to trial (Davies, Flin, and Baxter 1986, pp. 81-82). Children are questioned most often in relation to sexual molestation cases in which they may be the only witness able to give important information to the courts (Goodman et al. 1990, p. 249; Saywitz 1987, p. 36; Goodman and Schwartz-Kenney 1992, p. 17). Other children witness events such as intrafamily violence that adult perpetrators believed were unseen by others (Stafford 1962, p. 303). Stephen Goldsmith (1988) writes:

Ten years ago it was practically unheard of for a young child to testify in a criminal case. In recent years, however, children have become a regular source of information for police and prosecutors and an increasingly common sight on the witness stand. Prosecutors are called on daily to determine whether to pursue criminal charges when children relate accounts of physical or sexual abuse. (p. i)

TESTIMONY AND CHILDREN'S MEMORY

It appears that humankind has always had an interest in how memory operates and the conditions under which it is inaccurate. A logical consequence of this curiosity is how the desire to know how memory affects testimony.

Children's Recall Compared to Adults

Most research points to age as a major determinant of recall ability. Children, especially young children, provide less information on free recall than do adults. Recognizing the difference between quantity and quality of information is important; research has not shown that children's accounts are less accurate than those provided by adults, just that there is substantially less information recalled. Some scholars, on the other hand, argue that children's reports are both weak and inaccurate: "The reports of children are in every way inferior to those of adults: the range is small [and] the inaccuracy large . . ." (Whipple 1909, p. 162).

One researcher (Saywitz 1987, p. 42) exposed third, sixth, and ninth/tenth graders to an audiotaped story about a theft and asked for free recall afterwards. The youngest subjects recalled significantly fewer details about the event than either of the two older groups. Of interest, Saywitz (p. 45) reports that the third graders were able to use "recognition cues" to help them reconstruct the event and remember details they had not provided during free recall. In fact, they effectively increased their recall to the levels present in both older groups (p. 45).

Other researchers have found age effects on the amount of recall. Hilary Ratner and her associates (Ratner, Smith, and Dion 1986,

p. 423) found that adults were much better than kindergartners on free recall regarding details about what happened during a session in which they played with clay. Similarly, Stephen Ceci and his associates (Ceci, Ross, and Toglia 1987b, p. 46) found that adults' performance was so high on one memory task that they had to exclude the adults' answers from the comparisons. In a study comparing young children's recall, Gail Goodman and Christine Aman (1990, p. 1863) found that five-year-olds remembered significantly more information than three-year-olds about a session during which they played games with a male confederate. In short, researchers have consistently reported that children's performance on free recall is poorer than adults' and that recall ability increases with age.

Children are also less able to correctly answer direct questions about events. In one study, Ronald Cohen and Mary Anne Harnick (1980, p. 204) showed children a short film depicting the theft of a purse and a shoplifting incident and then asked them a set of specific questions about what they saw. The nine-year-olds were significantly less likely to correctly answer the questions when compared to the twelve-year-olds and adults.

Gail Goodman and Rebecca Reed (1986, p. 324) exposed children and adults to a scenario in which they interacted with a male confederate for five minutes and were then asked seventeen objective questions about the session (for example, "Did the man have a ring on?" or "What color was the man's hair?"). The mean number of questions answered correctly was highest for adults, then six-year-olds, then three-year-olds, but the differences between six-year-olds and adults were not significant. Both groups, however, performed significantly better than the three-year-olds.

Taken together, these studies point to age as a strong factor in the memory of children. Saywitz's (1987) findings about rehabilitation of recall, however, indicate that children's performance levels on free recall may be increased substantially.

Face Recognition

Accurate testimony by adults or children depends in part on witnesses' ability to remember events. Young children have been shown to be able to recognize faces as well as adults, a task very similar to choosing suspects from books of photographs or lineups. Barbara Marin and her associates (Marin et al. 1979, pp. 297-298), for example, presented kindergarten/first graders, third/fourth graders, seventh/eighth graders, and college students with a six-photo lineup from which to identify a male confederate who had entered the study laboratory and been involved in a brief altercation with the experimenter.[5] The four groups of subjects did not differ significantly with respect to accuracy; roughly 57 percent of the subjects were able to correctly identify the confederate.

In later research, Janat Parker and her colleagues (Parker, Haverfield, and Baker-Thomas 1986, pp. 290-292) showed adults and elementary-school children (mean age = 8 years) one of four sequences of fifteen color slides of a picnic scene in which seven people participated in a variety of activities. On the eleventh slide, a male entered the scene and stole a radio from a blanket; the thief was also visible in the next three slides.[6] Following the slide sequence, the subjects were asked to identify the suspect from a photographic lineup of six frontal-view photographs. The children and adults were equally accurate in this task (about one-half of the subjects were able to correctly identify the thief), although the children were more likely to change their initial choice when asked on retest to select the suspect (p. 299).[7]

Gail Goodman and Rebecca Reed (1986, pp. 321-323; also reported in Goodman, Hepps, and Reed 1986) exposed three- and six-year-old children and college students to a five-minute interaction with a male confederate. During the interaction, the subjects were directed in the performance of several hand and arm movements. Four or five days after the session, the subjects were presented with a five-photo lineup and asked to identify the confederate. The six-year-olds had the highest mean identification accuracy, followed by the adults, and then the three-year-olds (p. 326). Other results indicate that adults incorporated more suggested, but incorrect, details into their free recalls of the event, followed by six-year-olds, and then than three-year-olds (p. 326).[8]

When Children Outperform Adults in Memory Tasks

Children can remember as much as or more than adults when the situation is one with which they are very familiar. Michellene Chi

(1978, p. 82), for instance, found that young chess players (mean age = 10.5 years) were able to recall chess positions briefly presented to them better than adults unfamiliar with the game.[9] Additionally, Marc Lindberg (1980, p. 407) found that nine-year-olds recalled more than twenty-year-old college students when asked to recall thirty "third grade generated" words that were read to them; the words were generated by their classmates and included games they played, television characters from *Charlie's Angels* (a television show with three female protagonists that investigate and solve crimes),[10] buildings and teachers at their school, and material from books they read and cartoons they watched.[11] Chi's and Lindberg's work have implications for the legal community in that children may be able to outperform their adult counterparts when remembering situations which are well-known to children, such as school activities and play situations, among other possibilities.

Stephen Lepore (1990, p. 83) mentions the possibility that children may develop a knowledge base for repeated experiences like chronic sexual or physical abuse. Considering this possibility, a second implication of work like that of Chi and Lindberg may be that children's memory for this type of experience (repeated or chronic events) may improve as the event becomes more routine and familiar to them.

Some scholars have found that school-aged children can perform as well as teenagers when recalling stories. H.B.L. Vos (1911) read a story to children ages nine to fourteen (N = 800) and asked for free recall three days later. He found that the nine- and ten-year-olds remembered more than the thirteen- and fourteen-year-olds, and that the boys' recollections were better than the girls'.[12] It is also useful to note the method used in this early study on children's recall abilities (i.e., read a story and later ask for recall), since a great deal of later studies utilized this same methodology.

More recently, Karen Saywitz (1987, p. 44) found that third graders (mean age = 8.25 years) were able to effectively remember as much correct information from an audiotaped story about a theft as were sixth (mean age = 11.5 years) and ninth/tenth graders (mean age = 15 years).[13] This research shows that courts' fears of poorer recall by preadolescents compared to their elders may be unfounded.

Children sometimes outperform adults when asked to remember peripheral details. For example, in one study of selective looking and memory, children surpassed their adult counterparts when asked to recall a woman with an umbrella who walked across the court during a videotaped basketball game; three-fourths of first graders remembered the woman, but only a fifth of the adults did (Neisser 1979, pp. 215, 217). Marc Lindberg (1991, p. 53) found that third-graders were better able than sixth-graders and adults to recall details of a dialogue that was not central to a film about some cheating students. The subjects had been told to pay attention to the students in the film, but questions were later asked about the teacher's instructions.

When asked to remember if a telephone and/or rug were present in a room where they had played a game several days before, three- and six-year-old children performed significantly better than college students (Goodman and Reed 1986, p. 325). Similarly, Stephen Ceci and his associates (Ceci, Ross, and Toglia 1987b, experiment 4) report that preschoolers were somewhat better than college students at recognizing the name and hometown of a research confederate[14] two days after the confederate casually told them this information as part of a session following a story reading.

Kindergartners have been found to perform as well as adults in the recall of superordinate information, that is, general versus specific information (Ratner, Smith, and Dion 1986, p. 423).[15] For example, "I went to school" is superordinate information, while specific or subordinate information includes details of the activity, such as "I put a puzzle together at school" or "The teacher read us a story at school." Subordinate information was reported more often by adults in the study.

EARLY RESEARCH ON RECALL

Children have been called adequate observers, although they may be unable to recall some information correctly. According to Whipple (1912), one early researcher on children's memory (Heindl 1909), exposed children to a stranger for four minutes and then asked them to describe the person. In another test, children were asked to describe a well-known person who had not been presented to them.

Heindl found that "children are perfectly good observers, perhaps more objective than adults, but cannot translate their observations into [accurate reports]" (Whipple 1912, pp. 267-268). One of Heindl's conclusions, for example, was that the children overestimated the height of the stranger by three to five inches on average.

Children have not been shown to be universally inaccurate in their testimony. According to Whipple (1911, p. 308), H. Gross (1910) reacted to claims by some researchers that children's testimony should be excluded from the "court record whenever possible." Gross felt that researchers were generalizing from a few cases of inaccuracy when stating that all children are inaccurate in their recall from memory. He conceded that children do make errors in recall, but reminded researchers that adults, too, are inaccurate. Gross argued that a "healthy half-grown boy is the best possible witness for simple events" (Whipple 1911, p. 308), and cited some reasons why children may make better witnesses than adults: "freedom from prejudice, erroneous interpretation, emotion, intoxication, etc." (Whipple 1911, p. 308).

The disagreement by researchers as to children's ability to accurately testify about what they have seen led Guy Whipple (1911, p. 308) to suggest that "the whole matter could be very simply cleared up by an appropriate experiment. Why not subject observers of different ages to a graded series of event-tests?"[16] If only understanding the many multifaceted effects on children's testimony were that easy!

SUMMARY

In summary, researchers agree that younger children, especially toddlers, recall less about witnessed events than adults and older children. Note that this does not mean that the accuracy of children's reports is necessarily low. The few items children provide on free recall tend to be highly accurate. Adults, on the other hand, seem better able to provide a larger quantity of information than children, but the information may be less accurate. Errors seem more likely to creep into adults' accounts.

The research about children's memory and testimony also indicates that children are reasonably accurate when selecting pictures in simulated photo lineups. It is important to note, however, that these findings have been for target-present lineups (i.e., those where a picture of the perpetrator/confederate has been included among the sample of photos from which the child has been asked to select the correct picture). As will be seen in future chapters of this book, findings for target-absent lineups (i.e., those where the target picture is not included) differ because children sometimes select a picture although the correct picture is not included.

Research also shows that young children's memories are not always inferior to those of older children and adults. When familiarity with an event is high, children's recall abilities may be quite high. Instead of age, it may be the level of understanding individuals have for an event that determines how much they remember about what transpired. Since adults customarily understand more than children, it should come as no surprise that their recall usually surpasses that of children exposed to the same event. When children are at an advantage (for example, when the material to be recalled comes from things that normally occur in "children's spheres" such as the stories they know, the shows they watch, and the games they play), their recall abilities may exceed that of adults.

Finally, research shows that ability to remember peripheral details may be higher for children than for adults. It first, this finding is quite perplexing. It is possible that young children have some difficulty sorting out "useful" from "less valuable" material and attempt to encode everything they see and hear due to their reduced level of experience in selecting which information is important to remember. Consider, for example, how long it takes for students to learn how to take effective notes to help them study in their courses. Once the skill is learned, however, they are generally able to take notes in any course. Adults, who are better able to organize the information in the world around them, should have higher recall for what other adults consider important.

The next chapter will examine the effects of stress, prompting, and imagination on children's recall abilities.

Chapter 2

The Effects of Stress, Prompting, and Imagination on Children's Recall

Much of the testimony children provide in court is unlike the free recall sessions that commonly take place in memory studies. The event about which the testimony is being elicited may involve some stress, for example, or children may be prompted through specific questions about the event. This chapter will examine the effects that these and other questioning realities may have on the accuracy of children's testimony.

THE EFFECTS OF STRESS ON REMEMBERING

The effects of stress on children's ability to testify are of concern to the courts since many events about which children are called upon to testify are of a stressful nature. If the presence of stressors affects children's ability to remember, either in a positive way by increasing recall ability or in a negative way by acting as an impediment to recall, the effects need to be understood. The effects of stress on the memory of children has recently received increased attention due to the development of new ways of experimentation that avoid human subjects problems. Researchers have discovered that they can use naturally occurring events in experiments, thereby avoiding the sticky problem of subjecting children to stress and/or trauma in the name of science. Dental and medical visits, for example, are two common events that have been used to help illuminate the effects of stress on memory.

Gail Goodman and her colleagues (Goodman, Hepps, and Reed 1986, p. 171) found that stressed and nonstressed three- to seven-year-olds did not differ in their accuracy when asked a set of objective questions about their visit to a medical clinic three or four days after the incident. When the questioning was analyzed by level of salience, however, differences between the two groups emerged. The stressed children (who had received an inoculation during their visits) were more accurate when the questions dealt with salient information versus peripheral information. The nonstressed children (who only had decals rubbed on their arms by the laboratory technician), on the other hand, were more accurate on questions that dealt with peripheral information. Neither finding was significant, however, probably due to the small (N = 18) sample size (p. 171).

In a second inoculation study with more (N = 48) subjects, Goodman and her colleagues (1990, study 3; also reported in Goodman, Hirschman, Hepps, and Rudy 1991, study 2) found that stressed children recalled more information than other children. When the three- to six-year-old children were asked for free recall of their visits to a medical clinic three to nine days before, the most stressed children gave the most complete and accurate reports.[1] Children whose parents reported that they were very anxious before their inoculation were more accurate in identifying, from a six-photo lineup, the picture of the nurse who inoculated them (Goodman, Hirschman, Hepps, and Rudy 1991, p. 132).

In a third inoculation study, Goodman and her colleagues (Goodman, Hirschman, Hepps, and Rudy 1991, study 3) matched new control subjects (on age, sex, and treatment group) to a subset of the stressed children from their previous inoculation study (Goodman, Hirschman, Hepps, and Rudy 1991, study 2).[2] The stressed children recalled less incorrect information during free recall of the event when compared to the nonstressed control group. Although there were no significant differences between stressed and nonstressed groups for recall of correct information during recall, the authors note:

> These findings seem inconsistent with those of experiment 2 until it is realized that no children from Study 2 with a stress rating of 6 [the highest possible] were included in Study 3. Given that it was only these children who evidenced the beneficial effects of stress on memory, it is not surprising that few

differences emerged. (Goodman, Hirschman, Hepps, and Rudy 1991, p. 140)

In summary, the three studies by Goodman and her colleagues (Goodman, Hirschman, Hepps, and Rudy 1991) indicate that the presence of stress during an event may have positive effects on children's abilities to later testify accurately about what happened. It is interesting to note from the first of the three studies that the addition of stress to an event may effectively move children to concentrate more on salient, as opposed to peripheral information during recall.

Not all researchers agree that stress improves children's recall. Douglas Peters (1987; also reported in Peters 1991a, study 1), for example, asked three- to eight-year-olds to identify, from a five-photo lineup, the dentist and dental assistant present during their appointment one/two days or three/four weeks after a dental visit. The most stressed children[3] were significantly less able to correctly identify the dentist and dental assistant.[4] When asked to identify the dental room, however, there were no significant differences.

In another study by Peters (1991a, study 2), three- to six-year-olds at a nursery school had their pulse taken by a male confederate and were asked casual questions (for example, "What's your favorite TV show?"). During the session, half of the children's heads were "vigorously rubbed . . . until they attempted to avoid the rubbing by flinching their heads away or verbally protesting" (Peters 1991a, p. 63). Anxiety ratings were obtained for each child using Glennon and Weisz's Preschool Observational Scale of Anxiety. When asked to identify the man who took their pulse, the more anxious children were significantly less able to make a correct identification.[5]

A third study by Peters (1991a, study 3) found no significant differences between stressed three- to nine-year-olds versus non-stressed children who had been asked to recall twelve characteristics of a nurse (for example, color and length of hair) who had interacted with them one or ten to fourteen days earlier. The stressed group had received an inoculation, while the control group received a short talk about immunizations. When asked to identify the nurse in a five-photo lineup, the stressed children were significantly less able to make a correct identification.[6]

A fourth study by Peters (1991a, study 4) manipulated stress both at the time of encoding (storage of information into memory) and identification. Five- to ten-year-olds were left in a room with a money box containing about twenty dollars, while the interviewer and parents briefly left the room. While the child was alone, a male confederate entered the room and took the box. For the nonstressed group, the interviewer told the child before leaving the room that the research assistant would come to get the box; for the stressed group, however, the taking was staged as a theft, with the confederate acting surprised to see the room occupied, temporarily distracting the child, clandestinely taking the box, and noisily running out of the room. The interviewer and parent returned and asked what had happened to the box; after being told by the child that it was stolen, the interviewer ran down the hallway in search of the suspect and returned with five photos or five live men. The child was then asked to identify the culprit. For the nonstressed condition, both live and photo lineups were used, but the children were told it was a memory game to see if they could remember the research assistant who took the box. Children in the theft condition were significantly more stressed than those in the nontheft condition, and children were significantly more stressed during the live lineup than for the photo lineup. Children in the theft condition appeared to be affected by the live lineup and were less likely to make a correct identification.

A final study by Peters (1991a, study 5) tried to lead six- to nine-year-old children into believing a fire was in the building in which the children were being questioned. After having their body weight, blood pressure, and pulse measures taken, the children were asked casual questions (for example, "What is your favorite food?"). During the questioning, either (1) a fire alarm began to sound or (2) a radio was turned on, then a female confederate came into the room and either (1) acted concerned about a fire and looked out a window or (2) looked out the window to see if a delivery truck was outside. After the confederate left, the fire alarm or radio was turned off. Children in the fire-alarm condition were significantly less likely to make a correct identification when asked to select the confederate's picture from a six-photo lineup.

In contrast to Peters' (1991a) repeated findings that stressed children perform at a lower level than nonstressed children in photo recognition tasks, Gail Goodman (Goodman, Aman, and Hirschman 1987, p. 17) found no differences between stressed and nonstressed children on a six-photo lineup. The three- to seven-year-old children were either inoculated (stressed) or had a decal rubbed on their arms (nonstressed). Either three to four or seven to nine days later, the children were asked to identify the nurse who had inoculated them. A significant effect for age was found, with younger children performing at lower levels, but no significant effects for stress level were found. In contrast to Peters, Goodman assigned children to either stressed or nonstressed groups. All of Peters' subjects, however, were exposed to the treatment (here, a dental visit), with division into stressed and nonstressed groups made ex post facto based on anxiety ratings during the treatment. Also, Peters failed to control for age in his group assignments.

The effect of stress on children's testimony is unclear. The work by Peters shows that the ability of children to recognize faces may be impaired by the presence of a stressor. This position has not been without criticism. In a commentary to Peters' (1991a) article, Goodman (1991, p. 78-79) proposed that Peters' findings were due to factors other than the stress level of the children. For the first two studies, Goodman noted that the more stressed children tended to be younger than the nonstressed children (this relationship was significant) and the performance of younger children on photo recognition is known to be poorer than that of older children. Goodman also argued that the more stressed children may not have looked at the dentist or assistant due to their fear. Then, for Peters' study number 3, Goodman noted that the rooms for the children receiving inoculations were different from the room used to deliver the short talk to the control group.

In a rebuttal to Goodman's (1991) commentary, Peters (1991b, p. 90) attacks the idea that his results were due to anything other than stress level: "If Goodman really wants us to believe that high levels of stress facilitate children's recollections, then . . . considerably better studies than hers are going to be necessary to prove this point." Peters cites three contemporary studies as having findings consistent with his own findings that when stress has an impact on children's memory, it is negative (Vandermass 1991; Ornstein, Gordon, and Larus 1992;[7] Leippe, Romanczyk, and Manion 1991).

Research by Goodman and her associates, on the other hand, shows that stress level may actually enhance children's abilities to recall what happened to them or what they saw. The reasons for these differences may also lie in the methodology used; Peters' work centers on photo lineups, while Goodman's typically focuses on ability to recall what happened.[8] It is possible that this and other differences in their methodologies drives their findings.

Stressed children may remember certain facts about their experiences very well, but fail to focus their attention on all pieces of information associated with the event. As an analogy, nearly all women remember much about the birth of their first child even after several decades, but are unable to describe the hospital room or nurses in attendance, since those details may have been unimportant to the new mother. When Goodman and her colleagues (Goodman et al. 1990, Study 3) questioned the inoculated children, those facts that the children remembered were very important to them. Had Goodman's subjects been asked to select their dentist from a photo-lineup, they may have been unable to do so, since the dentist may not have been the focus of their attention.[9] Indeed, Goodman (1991, p. 78) alludes to this in her commentary to Peters' (1991a) article: "[the children may have] closed their eyes, stared at the ceiling lights and dental instruments and generally looked away from the dentist."[10]

Research findings regarding stress and children's memory suggest to courts that while stress may enhance recall of certain types of facts, it may also decrease children's attention to other stimuli present during an event. Children who have witnessed stressful events may be less accurate witnesses, but more research on the effects of stress on children's witness capabilities is necessary before these effects can be fully understood.

PROMPTING

Very young children sometimes require more prompts when questioned, that is, their free recall ability suffers; they may not be able to recall facts without some outside prompting to refresh their memories (Graham 1985, p. 230; Ratner, Smith, and Dion 1986, p. 425). Prompting may be one way to improve a preschooler's memory.

Some recent research has pointed to the ability of children to recall as much as adults when properly cued (Melton 1981, p. 82). Gail Goodman and Rebecca Reed (1986, p. 324), for example, found that there were no significant differences in accuracy between six-year-olds and adults when asked a set of seventeen objective questions[11] about a five-minute interaction with a male confederate.[12]

It is important to distinguish prompting from leading questions. Prompting differs from leading questions in both the amount of information provided to the witness and the wording used: a leading question "implies the answer," whereas prompting is "specific, yet nonleading" (Bull 1992, pp. 9-10). For purposes of the courts, prompting may include questions which may help the child remember certain details, such as "What happened next?" or "What color was the man's jacket?" (if the child has already mentioned a man wearing a jacket).[13] Prompting may help focus children's attention on details they may have overlooked during free recall.

While prompting may decrease the differences between adults and children on memory tasks, the change may simply result from reducing the memory tasks from recall to recognition. As previously discussed, children often perform better on recognition tasks. When properly conducted, then, prompting may serve to reduce the differences in accuracy between children and adult witnesses when testifying about an event. When improperly conducted, however, prompting is the same as questioning with leading questions.

THE EFFECT OF PROPS

Some children may require "concrete retrieval cues" to jog their memories (Goodman 1984b, p. 163). Questioning techniques utilizing props have been successfully used to elicit details from children. Children who are having difficulty recalling an event may benefit from the use of props or other nonverbal techniques, especially those who do not possess developed verbal skills (Faller 1984, p. 478; King and Yuille 1987, p. 31).

Goodman (1984b, p. 162) reports that D.W.W. Price (1984) found that the recall of four-year-old children increased substantially when they were presented with a small model of the playroom they had visited earlier.[14] While recall for two-and-a-half-year-old subjects did not increase with the use of the model, their recall rose dramatically when they were placed back in the actual room. This finding does not mean that "concrete retrieval cues" are not useful with toddlers. Instead, it appears to show that props may be most useful with children who are able to comprehend that models are small replicas of actual places or objects. Refreshing younger children's memories may require visiting the places for which the models are made.

Of interest, Price (1984) reported that none of his subjects resorted to fantasy in their reenactment of events when they were questioned using props. This finding is important to the legal community in that the utilization of props may provide for more accurate testimony, not only in terms of higher recall, but also in a way that helps prevent children from exercising their own possibly imaginative ideas about what happened.[15]

Even less realistic props may be useful when children are providing legally relevant statements. Richard Thomas (1956), in a law review article on child witnesses, wrote about a case in which a child was hit by an automobile. One of the witnesses, a playmate of the injured child,[16] was unable to tell the attorney much,

> [b]ut when he was invited to pretend that a nearby object was the building next to which the accident occurred, and was given a toy automobile and some toy soldiers to use he was able to give an accurate demonstration of what had happened. (Thomas 1956, p. 220)

Thomas suggests that this style of testifying is more accurate than that obtained through the use of leading questions. Further, it is likely that juries hearing testimony obtained through the use of props would be less likely to attribute the testimony to coaching or susceptibility to suggestive questions.

According to Mary Ann King and John Yuille (1987, p. 31), another benefit of utilizing props when questioning children is the ability to minimize "confusion in communication." When asked questions by adults, young children experience some confusion; for example, when an adult repeats a question already answered by the child, the child may believe the first answer was inappropriate and may change his or her answer in order to please the adult. The largely nonverbal nature of recreating the event using props may help reduce the effects of this type of confusion.

CHILDREN AND REALITY MONITORING

A concept related to memory of children is "reality monitoring" (Johnson and Raye 1981). Stephan Lindsay and Marcia Johnson (1987, p. 92) state that a person's own memory for an event may be confused with memories of what others have said about the event. Children, like adults, are sometimes unable to discriminate between sources of memories. Elizabeth Loftus (1979, p. 62) cites the classic example of psychologist Jean Piaget, who remembered, in very rich detail, his own kidnapping as a two-year-old child. Later it was found that his nurse had fabricated the story; Piaget's vivid memory was of a nonexistent event suggested to him by his nurse:

> I was sitting in my pram . . . when a man tried to kidnap me. I was held in by the strap fastened round me while my nurse bravely tried to stand between me and the thief. She received various scratches, and I can still see those on her face. Then a crowd gathered, a policeman with a short cloak and a white baton came up, and the man took to his heels. I can still see the whole scene, and can even place it near the tube station. (Piaget 1962, pp. 187-188)

The ability to differentiate between what one witnessed and what others have said about the event is important because those who are unable to make such distinctions make poor witnesses. A common worry in the courtroom is that a child may confuse memories of actual occurrences with fantasy or events that were only imagined by the child. As one law review article stated:

Often the child intermingles imagination with memory, with resulting damage to the opposing party. Thus falsehood can be irretrievably engraved on the record by a most convincing and guileless witness with no conception that it is wrong to say the words spoken. (Collins and Bond 1953, p. 105)

Research has shown that children are able to differentiate between events they imagine and the concrete actions of another person. Marcia Johnson and Mary Ann Foley (1984) conducted a series of experiments to see if children would confuse memories of witnessed events with imagined images. In the first experiment, children (eight-, ten-, and twelve-year-olds) were no more likely than adults to confuse the number of times a slide was shown with the number of times a slide was imagined. For this experiment, subjects were shown a series of slides and asked to imagine viewing the same series of slides. The slides were shown once, twice, or three times, while the slides were imagined once, three times, or not at all. Following the session, the subjects were asked to judge how many times each slide was shown. Subjects answered that slides which had been shown most frequently appeared most often, regardless of the number of times the slide was imagined (1984, p. 41).

A second experiment (Johnson and Foley 1984) showed that six- and nine-year-olds were as capable as seventeen-year-olds in remembering if they had said a word or if someone else had said the word. The subjects were asked to say a list of words and heard someone else say another list of words. After the session, they were asked if they had said the word, if someone else had said the word, or if the word was a new one which neither person had said. The authors also found that while nine- and seventeen-year-olds were able to distinguish whether they had said a word or only imagined themselves saying the word, six-year-olds were less able to do so.[17]

In a third experiment (Johnson and Foley 1984), six-year-olds were compared with nine-year-olds with respect to their abilities to discriminate sources of words. Results indicate that the younger children were just as capable as their older counterparts in distinguishing: (1) words they had said from words others had said; (2) which of two other people had said a word; and (3) if they had thought about a word or heard someone else say it. The six-year-olds, however, were less capable of distinguishing whether they had said a word or only imagined themselves saying it.

In their fourth experiment, Johnson and Foley (1984) found that six- and nine-year-old children were as capable as college students in distinguishing their actions from the actions of another person and which actions each of two other actors performed. They were, however, less capable of distinguishing their own actions from actions they had only imagined themselves doing.[18]

Johnson and Foley's (1984) findings point to the capability of children to accurately testify about events involving others–a finding of concern to courts in deciding whether or not another person did an act to a child or if the child only imagined the activity. What is less certain, however, is whether children can accurately recount events involving their own actions; children may imagine themselves performing an action and report the imagined activity as an actual happening. This later finding should not be overly disconcerting to the courts in cases where children are reporting the activities of others. When they are testifying about their own actions, on the other hand, the possibility is higher that children may incorporate their imaginations into their accounts.

A concern often raised by advocates for the defense in allegations of child abuse is that the child is fantasizing about sexual abuse and reporting the fantasy as truth. Along these lines, Patricia Morison and Howard Gardner (1978, p. 648) report that kindergartners and second-, fourth-, and sixth-graders were able to separate fantasy from reality. For example, two fantasy-based image-bearing cards (e.g., witch and genie) should be paired together by the children because, as the youngsters put it, "they are not real," as opposed to the witch being paired with a broom because "a witch flies on a broom" (Morison and Gardner 1978, p. 645). Further, when asked to classify twenty cards into two piles ("one pile of things that are real and one pile of things that are pretend") and to describe why each card belonged in the pile to which it was assigned, even kindergartners correctly classified most of the cards, although level of accuracy increased with age.[19] The researchers point out that children's ability to distinguish reality from fantasy may even be underestimated by their study, since "children can frequently handle a distinction in practice before they demonstrate it in formal testing or describe it verbally" (Morison and Gardner 1978, p. 648). Morison and Gardner's research sheds some light on the potential of school-aged witnesses to accurately classify items as fact or fancy, but it may tell us little about children's ability to determine the difference between the two in practice. Children are often given conflicting information with expected results. A child, for example, may classify Santa Claus as fancy, but also report that he exists.

SUMMARY

What does the literature about children's memory and testimony tell us about children as witnesses? First, stress may improve children's recall of salient information at the expense of more peripheral details. Second, cuing and props may help jog the memory of children without suggesting answers and tainting their testimony. Third, while children can reliably distinguish between the actions of others and actions they only visualized others completing, pre-schoolers may report as fact events in which they only imagined they participated.

At present, more research on the effects of stress is needed in order to explain the contradictory findings of Goodman and Peters, who report that stress inhibits and improves memory. Particular attention should be paid to how the stress level is manipulated experimentally and to the similarity of the tasks the children are asked to complete. This area is one of the most important directions for research on children's testimony, given that testimony is rarely elicited about events that are neutral or calm for children.

Children are probably unlikely to fabricate and report crimes by others (Johnson and Foley 1984, p. 45), in particular sexual acts of which they should have little knowledge. Kathleen Faller (1984, p. 475), for example, asserts that children do not make up stories about sexual abuse because it is not "in their interests" to do so and many children lack the sexual knowledge necessary to convince an adult that the abuse has taken place. Concern however, has arisen over attempts to prompt children to report crimes. The real fear is that children, when asked questions designed to uncover molestation (for example, "Did he touch your private parts?") may agree with the questioner whether or not the event actually occurred.

It is not the actual memory of children that has come under fire by recent critics, but rather, the ability of the child to accurately relay to the court the occurrences and/or events in question (Marin et al. 1979, p. 297). The prompting that is often necessary to assist children with eyewitness tasks may be leading and directly affect their testimony. This phenomenon, "suggestibility," is the subject of the next chapter.

Chapter 3

Suggestibility:
Is the Witness Telling the Truth
or Reacting to Suggestion?

After an event, witnesses are often exposed to information regarding what they saw or heard (Loftus and Davies 1984, p. 56). For example, individuals often talk to others about events they witnessed. This postevent information, correct or incorrect, may alter the witness's memory (Loftus and Davies 1984, p. 56; Yuille 1980, p. 336). When this happens, the witness is referred to as "suggestible."

ADULTS AND SUGGESTIBILITY

Suggestibility is not only a problem in child witnesses. Adult testimony can also be tainted. In an early study conducted by Elizabeth Loftus and John Palmer (1974, p. 586), for example, college students were shown seven short films depicting automobile accidents. Following each film, the subjects were asked to provide a free recall account of the accident and then were asked to estimate the speed at which the cars were traveling when they hit each other. For some subjects, different words (smashed, collided, bumped, and contacted) were substituted for the word "hit." Results showed that the postevent information (here, the wording of the question) significantly impacted on the estimates of automobile speeds, with "smashed" and "collided" receiving the highest estimates and "contacted" receiving the lowest.[1]

In a second experiment (Loftus and Palmer 1974, p. 587), college students were shown a short film depicting a multiple-car accident.

Following the film, the subjects were asked to provide an account of the accident and to answer a questionnaire. The critical question again involved the speed of the automobiles: one-third of the subjects were asked how fast the cars were going when they "smashed" into each other, one-third were asked how fast the cars were going when they "hit" each other, and the remaining third were not asked for any estimate of the automobiles' speed. One week later, the subjects were asked if they had seen any broken glass (there was no broken glass in the film). Again, the wording of the question significantly impacted upon the estimates: those who were questioned using "smashed" gave higher speed estimates and were more likely to state that they had seen glass.

A later study (Loftus and Zanni 1975, p. 87) exposed graduate students to a short film depicting a multiple-car accident. Following the film, the subjects provided a free recall of the accident and answered a twenty-two item questionnaire containing six target items (three of the questions pertained to items present in the film and three pertained to items not present in the film). One-half of the subjects were asked questions using an indefinite article (for example, "Did you see *a* stop sign?"); the other half received questions using a definite article (for example, "Did you see *the* stop sign?"). Subjects were significantly more likely to answer "yes" when the question was phrased using a definite article.

Another experiment (Loftus and Zanni 1975, experiment 2, p. 87) was identical to the first except for a change in the film and the population. People in a public library (aged fourteen to twenty) were shown a short film depicting a minor collision between a car backing out of a parking space in a parking lot and a pedestrian carrying a bag of groceries. Again the subjects were asked to provide a free recall of the accident and answer a twenty-two item questionnaire containing six target items. The six target questions again differed in their use of a definite versus indefinite article. Results showed that subjects were significantly more likely to answer affirmatively when the question which asked whether certain facts were true was phrased using a definite article (for example, "Did you see *the* stop sign?"). This was true even when the questions asked about nonexistent items (p. 88).

A number of other studies by Loftus and her colleagues have found results similar to the studies presented here: postevent information has consistently been shown to affect memory. One study, for example, found effects on memory for passive versus aggressive wording of questions (Loftus, Altman, and Geballe 1975, pp. 163-164). A videotape depicting the disruption of a class by eight demonstrators was shown to college students. Target questions were either passive (for example, "Did the professor *say* anything . . .") or aggressive (for example, "Did the professor *shout* anything . . ."). One week later, the subjects were asked to answer a series of questions about the video. Subjects who were asked aggressive target questions felt the incident was, among other things, noisier and more violent, than those exposed to passive wording.

Another Loftus study (Loftus, Miller, and Burns 1978, p. 30) reports that adults are vulnerable to suggestions regarding an auto-pedestrian accident. A total of five experiments were conducted using college students as subjects. The experiments involved a series of slides in which a car traveled along a side street, turned a corner, and hit a pedestrian. Manipulations included whether the car stopped at a STOP versus a YIELD sign (versus no mention of a sign) and whether a shovel or a pair of skis was leaning against a tree. Results for all five experiments indicated that postevent information changes recall of an event. It was also shown that longer periods between stimulus and questioning are related to poorer performance in recall (see also Loftus 1977).[2]

Possibly the most dramatic example of suggestibility in adults was discovered by some of Loftus' students outside of the laboratory and was discussed by Loftus (1979) in her book, *Eyewitness Testimony.* The assignment given to the students was to go and "create in someone's mind, a 'memory' for something that did not exist" (Loftus 1979, p. 61). One group of students staged a theft of a nonexistent tape recorder in several public places (for example, train stations). Two females would enter the public place and one of them would set down her bag. Both would walk away (for example, to look at the train schedules). A male would "lurk" over to the bag and pretend to stuff something under his coat before quickly leaving. The females would return, then the owner of the bag would notice that the bag had been disturbed and would cry out, "Oh my god, my tape recorder is missing!" (Loftus 1979, p. 62). The two women began to question nearby eyewitnesses, got their phone numbers, and had a confederate posing as an insurance agent call the eyewitnesses a week later. The eyewitnesses not only remembered the "theft" of the nonexistent tape recorder,[3] but were able to describe the recorder "in reasonably good detail" (Loftus 1979, p. 62).

Research by Loftus and her colleagues shows that adults are misled rather easily by questions and may have detailed memories for events that were merely suggested to them. Courts have long recognized that this phenomenon exists; it may explain, at least in part, the courts' desires for jurors who are unfamiliar with each case.

It is important to realize that Loftus' findings cannot be explained away as legally unimportant. Many of the questions she asked were presented from the viewpoint of someone representing the legal system. The description and speed of cars involved in auto accidents and the details of thefts are very appropriate arenas of inquiry for both the criminal and civil courts. Further, such questions are likely to fall within the domain of the witness, and may have a significant effect on the ultimate verdict.

CHILDREN AND SUGGESTIBILITY

Scholars have long doubted the ability of children to give truthful accounts of past events due to their suggestible nature. Children have been labeled as far more suggestible than adults, although there is a lack of scientific knowledge supporting that assumption (Zaragoza 1987, p. 53). Throughout this century, child suggestibility has been exploited in the courtroom, perhaps making children, as Babinsky (1910, translated in Whipple 1911, p. 308) noted "the most dangerous of all witnesses."[4] L. William Stern (1902, p. 55; see also Stern 1907-1908) argued that children are very susceptible to even the slightest of suggestions, and that even straightforward questions affect the accuracy of their accounts because they cannot think for themselves. This widely held opinion was supported and basically unquestioned by research of the time (Whipple 1909, p. 162). Today, children are assumed by many to be very suggestible, to the point of not being even remotely able to recount past events accurately (Ceci, Ross, and Toglia 1987b, p. 39; Goodman, Golding, and Haith 1984, p. 152).

EARLY RESEARCH

Guy Montrose Whipple credits Alfred Binet (Binet and Henri 1894; 1897; 1900; 1905; 1911) with "initiating the work in this [psychology of testimony] field" (Whipple 1911, p. 307). Binet researched the effects of suggestibility on children's testimony and found that children were very suggestible (Goodman 1984a, p. 19; Stern 1902, p. 53). He argued that children should not be questioned and that they should instead be required to write out their reports, a difficult task at best for most youngsters.

Whipple (1918, p. 245) reports that, on one occasion, Binet questioned children using nonsuggestive and suggestive questions. They correctly reported the events 74 percent of the time when questioned in a nonsuggestive manner, but their accuracy dropped to 62 percent when moderately suggestive questions were employed and plummeted to 39 percent when strongly suggestive questions were used. Children were viewed as able to give accurate testimony under some circumstances, but as very suggestible (Goodman 1984a, p. 22).

Whipple himself was no fan of children as witnesses. Based on research conducted by others, especially Binet, he denounced children as unable to testify in a truthful manner as to what they witnessed. He went beyond the idea that children incorporate into their testimony untrue elements presented to them by others and instead attributed the inaccuracies to the children themselves, furthering the opinion of a witness who was at best, unpredictable, and at worst, diabolic: "the child sees and hears and reproduces what he wants to see and hear and reproduce" (Whipple 1909, p. 163).

J. Varendonck (in his 1911 work translated by Hazan, Hazan, and Goodman 1984a) was extremely hostile toward the notion that children could be valuable witnesses. He was asked by the defense to write a report on the value of the testimony to be heard in the case of Van Puyenbroeck, a man accused of the murder and rape of a child. The central witnesses were nine-year-old Louise Van der Stuyft and Van Puyenbroeck's eight-year-old daughter, Elvire. Varendonck writes, "From my first reading of the record, I was convinced of poor Van Puyenbroeck's innocence. . . . The accusation was based solely on the testimony of children" (Varendonck 1911, translated in Goodman 1984a, p. 27). Varendonck bolstered his opinion with a description of his own experiments in which he presented misleading information to elementary school students:

> I succeeded in convincing the great majority of the students in my class, by nothing but pronouncing his name, that Monsieur M. came to see me in their presence. And these children described a person that they had not even seen. Can it be astonishing, consequently, that the name of the accused was obtained from Louise Van der Stuyft and Elvire Van Puyenbroeck? . . . Alone with my conscience, in the calm of my office, I finished expressing my profound conviction that the children who testified in his case had seen nothing, absolutely nothing of the murder, nor the murderer; and that consequently, we cannot set the least value in their declarations . . . children cannot observe . . . their suggestibility is inexhaustible . . . . We cannot trust the declarations of children when they claim to have observed certain details they describe. . . . Their imaginations play dirty tricks on them . . . . When are we going to give up, in all civilized nations, listening to children in courts of law?[5] (Varendonck 1911, translated in Goodman 1984a, pp. 27-31)

Ernest Dupré (1910) may have been one of the most outspoken critics of children's testimony. He noted that the value of a person's testimony increases with age and that "practically all that [children] say is erroneous" due to their "extreme suggestibility" (p. 355). Children make poor witnesses, Dupré argued, because their "psychological beings" are not yet fully developed and will not be fully developed until they reach adulthood: "So, the . . . child could be compared to the prehistorical human mind, like a modern specimen of paleopsychology" (p. 358). He also specifically warns the public to be wary of three categories of child liars (p. 361). The first, "false martyr children," have discovered a way of getting attention through telling lies that hurt others who often cannot adequately defend themselves against the child's charges of impropriety. The second group of children lies due to curiosity; Dupré reports that one girl, for example, admitted to fabricating a report of abuse because she wanted to experience the "luxurious" chairs a friend told her were in the local judge's chambers. The final group is comprised of those who falsely implicate others to conceal their own wrongdoing; one boy, for example, reported that a merchant attacked him as a way to explain why he came home late (p. 363). Dupré reports that there are "many" examples to substantiate his claims that children lie in court.

Dupré (1910, p. 356) blamed part of the suggestibility problem on society's attempts to foster within children strong imaginations, rather than focusing on training them to be accurate observers. He felt that we could attempt to counter the phenomenon by developing children's untapped skills as witnesses. Due to their increased levels of suggestibility in the meantime, however, he recommended against allowing children to testify in court:

> Their testimony, in general, does not merit the belief we are disposed to give it. It must be held as least true when it is coming from a young subject. The testimony of the child must be considered . . . as at least extremely suspect and must never be accepted unless only for the benefit of inventory and checking . . . . The magistrate should not, in any case, give any effective value to the testimony of a child. (Dupré 1910, pp. 366-367)

In 1914, T.H. Pear and Stanley Wyatt exposed ten- to fourteen-year-old children to a complex activity involving a man and a woman who entered the children's classrooms and interacted with the teacher. During the course of the interaction,[6] the man pulled various objects from a large bag he carried, showed them to the teacher while making comments such as "How do you like this?", positioned each object on the teacher's desk in view of the children, and at the conclusion of the interaction replaced the objects in his bag. The woman stood beside the man and "took some violets from her muff, rearranged them, and then replaced them" (Pear and Wyatt 1914, p. 393). The two then said goodbye and left the room; the children's class resumed as normal.

On the following day, the children were asked to write out a free recall of the incident, including everything they saw from the time the pair entered and left the classroom. The results indicated that the children's free recall was very reliable and accurate: "In many respects, not a single deviation was to be found. Thus, when the testimony of children is unaffected by questions or suggestions, it is worthy of the utmost consideration" (Pear and Wyatt 1914, p. 397).

However, after analyzing the children's answers to a set of direct questions of varying degrees of suggestion (for example, "On which part of [the man's] face was there a cut?" when there had been no cut), the authors were far less optimistic:

> Over one-third of the replies of normal children and over one-half of the replies of the mentally defectives[7] are incorrect. Thus, the interrogatory of the latter group is very unreliable and the corresponding testimony of the normal children must be treated with great reserve. (Pear and Wyatt 1914, p. 401)

As part of a larger study on the differences of sex and age on the reliability of testimony conducted for Japan's Ministry of Justice in 1939, Tadashi Uematsu administered picture-tests (Uematsu 1982, p. 153).[8] The researcher exposed four- and five-year-olds, eleven- to sixteen-year-olds, college students, middle-aged (forty to fifty years of age) adults, and elderly (over sixty) subjects to a complex picture about which questions would be asked later. Uematsu described what he did:

> In the presented picture, the eldest was a boy standing in the center of the sidecar wearing a white cap, blue coat, and he was holding a white handkerchief in his left hand. While, on his left side was seated a girl younger than him, wearing a red hat and a green dress, and on his right side was seen only the face of a girl, the youngest in age among them. What should be especially mentioned is that as the red color of the motorcycle occupied the main part of the picture, the color seemed to be very impressive to the hypothetical witnesses.
>
> Questions concerning this picture consisted of 39 items ranging from the color of the motorcycle and its license number to the looks, physique, age, clothes, personal effects, etc., of the driver and those of other persons having a ride on the car. (Uematsu 1982, p. 153)

The subjects were questioned after viewing the picture for about a minute. Some of the questions about the picture were suggestive (for example, the researcher asked about the driver's hairstyle, although the driver wore a cap that completely covered his hair). Questions were also asked about the experimenter himself, as he had spent about three minutes with the subjects while administering the picture-test. Tadashi Uematsu's conclusions regarding child witnesses were generally cynical:

> Infants are susceptible to suggestions and have a strong 'perseveration tendency', and at the same time, they often answer mechanically without prudency. Therefore, we must generally be careful in adopting what they say as evidence, but as there exists a large individual variation among them, their testimony can in some exceptional cases be very reliable. (Uematsu 1982, p. 154)

CURRENT RESEARCH
(1979 TO PRESENT)

More recent research has demonstrated that children's suggestibility may be quite limited (Ceci, Ross, and Toglia 1987b, p. 47; Goodman 1984b, p. 161; Goodman, Hirschman, and Rudy 1987; Loftus and Davies 1984, p. 63), and in some instances, children are not more vulnerable to suggestion than adults or older children (Duncan, Whitney, and Kunen 1982, p. 1218; Hoving, Hamm, and Galvin 1969, pp. 634-635; Marin et al. 1979, p. 303; Zaragoza 1987, p. 45).

Gail Goodman and Rebecca Reed (1986, p. 324) found that when incorrect information was "suggested about the central action" of a five-minute interaction with a male confederate, there were no significant differences between three- and six-year-olds or adults. When asked leading questions about minor details, however (for example, "Didn't the man wear glasses?"), adults were significantly less suggestible than the two younger groups. Of particular interest to courts, the six-year-olds were significantly less suggestible than the three-year-olds (p. 325). This finding may indicate that six-year-olds can resist suggestions when testifying in court, but that younger witnesses, such as the preschoolers in the McMartin case, may be more susceptible to leading questions.

Maria Zaragoza (1987, p. 66) tested three- and six-year-old subjects using her Control-Standard-Modified test procedure (see McCloskey and Zaragoza 1985, p. 4). Twenty-nine slides showing a story about a young girl riding her toy giraffe around a park were shown to the subjects, who were later exposed to biased or unbiased information about four of the slides, and then asked to choose which of two slides they had seen previously. The subjects were divided into three test groups. The Control group received no misinformation and then were asked to choose between correct and incorrect pictures. A second group (Standard) received misinformation that was followed by a choice between correct pictures and incorrect pictures which contained the misinformation. Finally, a third group (Modified) received misinformation followed by a choice between correct pictures and incorrect pictures which contained information that had not been suggested (in other words, the Modified group's incorrect pictures contained elements that had not been suggested, but were still incorrect). The reasoning behind this seemingly peculiar style of presentation is that subjects whose memories are distorted by the presentation of erroneous information should choose the picture containing the incorrect, but suggested, information. If, instead, subjects have actually forgotten the target information, they should choose the picture containing information they have not yet seen about half of the time. Finally, if subjects remember the original information, and know that the information suggested to them was incorrect, there is no demand characteristic operating to induce them to choose the information they know is incorrect.

Zaragoza (1987, p. 71) found that children in the Modified group performed almost identically on control items (those for which unbiased information was given) and misled items (those for which biased information was given). The subjects were accurate on roughly 70 percent of the items in both groups. The Standard group, however, performed significantly less accurately on misled items when compared to control items. While they were accurate on 77 percent of the control items, their rate fell to 54 percent for the misled items.

These results indicate that at least part of the error in children's recall is related to their accepting suggestions about incorrect information. Note that the suggestions were not effective, however, unless future questions involved a choice between the correct answer and an answer that contained the misleading suggestions. When a choice was given between the correct answer and an answer that contained new (unsuggested) information, the children performed as though no suggestion had been offered. This means that there is more than simply forgetting going on with respect to children's memory; there is a curious interrelationship between memory and type of suggestion. It also means that a few mistaken suggestions to children about what they did not actually witness need not necessarily taint their memories as long as future direct questions do not include the option to choose the incorrectly suggested information.

Zaragoza (1987, pp. 71-72) undertook a second experiment using a group who received no misinformation and a group who received misinformation followed by a choice between correct pictures and incorrect pictures which contained information that had not been suggested. Both groups were as able to correctly answer misleading items as items which were not misleading; roughly 74 percent of both types of choices were made correctly. These results led Zaragoza (1987, pp. 72-73) to state:

> Taken together, the results of both experiments support the idea that, at least in this situation, children's memories are just as resistant to forgetting as those of adults . . . . at this point, it can be concluded with some confidence that young children are not more suggestible than adults in all circumstances.

Edward Duncan and his associates (Duncan, Whitney, and Kunen 1982, p. 1218) found that the "relative influence" of suggestions equally impacted adults and first, third, and fifth graders. The subjects were shown a series of fourteen stories in slide format (each story contained seven to fourteen slides). Questions were designed to suggest alternative story plots. The authors, for example, described the story of a caveman who was out hunting with his friends when they were attacked by a bear. One of three types of questions were asked after the story: correct information ("When the bear appeared and broke the man's spear, where did it chase the men?"), incorrect information ("When the bear appeared and broke the man's fishing pole, where did it chase the men?"), and no information ("When the bear appeared, where did it chase the men?"). Later questions determined the effect of the question type on future answers (for example, "Were the men fishing when the bear appeared?"). A second analysis including only subjects who had demonstrated good factual memory for the event,[9] however, found that first graders "were unaffected by either correct or misleading information whereas the older subjects were significantly affected by both information types" (Duncan, Whitney, and Kunen 1982, p. 1218).

These results may point to a lack of suggestibility in children who have strong memories for events they have witnessed. It appears, given findings by Duncan and his colleagues (1982), that it is those children with poor memories for what they have seen who are the most dangerous witnesses when questioned suggestively. Of course, it may be difficult to assess the strength of a given witness' memory for an event if the child is the only one who saw what happened. Future research, then, should explore whether "good" memories generalize from one event to another. Is it possible, for example, to test children's accuracies using a planned event (for which adults know the answers to questions) in order to help predict their performance on questions about the actual event they witnessed? It is also possible that the amount of information and the level of detail provided by child witnesses on free recall tasks indicates the "strength" of their memories for what they have seen or heard.

In a study designed to assess the impact of suggestions made *before* an event, Ann Brown and her colleagues (Brown et al. 1977, experiment 1) found that suggestibility increased with age. Third-, fourth-, and seventh-grade subjects were exposed to an audiotaped story, for which they received one of two "orientations." The orientation consisted of telling the subjects that they would hear a story about "George, an escaped convict" or "Galen . . . of the *Planet of the Apes* television series" (Brown et al. 1977, p. 1456). The third graders were significantly less likely than the older children to incorporate suggestions into their free recall of the story (p. 1459).[10]

In a second experiment, Brown and her colleagues found that exposing second, fourth, and sixth graders to information regarding a passage from a story before the child is exposed to the passage can affect their free recall ability differentially (Brown et al. 1977,

p. 1464). In this study, the subjects were exposed to the suggestive information through listening to one of three stories about the fictitious "Targa" tribe one week before hearing the passage about which questions would be asked. One story depicted the Targa as Eskimos, one showed them as desert Indians, and one discussed nothing about the Targa (this control group heard about the Spanish instead of the Targa). A week after this treatment, the subjects were read the target passage and questioned about its contents. Those subjects exposed to information that depicted the Targa as Eskimos were more likely to incorporate intrusions such as "cold" and "icy" into their free recalls, while those exposed to information depicting the Targa to be desert Indians were more likely to incorporate intrusions such as "hot" and "sand" into their free recalls. The study also found that when intrusions occurred, the "older children's intrusions were [significantly] more likely to be theme related than younger children's" (Brown et al. 1977, p. 1462). The older children were again more affected by suggestions about the Targa.

From the research of Brown and her colleagues, we learn that older subjects may be more likely to incorporate suggestions into their statements due to selective judgment about events based on their existing knowledge. It appears that younger children, due at least in part to their reduced lack of experience, are less likely to "miscode" information when they witness it. Consider, for example, Robert Buckhout's (1974, p. 26) finding that some witnesses described a person who came into their classes as a black man despite the fact that the interloper was completely covered by a bag that prevented witnesses from see any part of him. This inaccuracy is presumably due more to the witnesses' own previous experiences or prejudices than to what they actually saw.[11] Children, then, may be less likely to selectively remember what they have seen due to their reduced level of prejudice.

Research on children's suggestibility is far from conclusive. Ronald Cohen and Mary Anne Harnick (1980, p. 204) showed children a twelve-minute black-and-white film depicting the theft of a purse and a shoplifting incident. Following the film, the subjects were asked both specific questions (for example, "What was the young woman carrying when she entered the bus?") and suggestive questions (for example, "The woman was carrying a newspaper when she entered the bus, wasn't she?" when she had actually been carrying a shopping bag).[12] Nine-year-old subjects were significantly more likely to accept false suggestions than twelve-year-olds or adults.[13]

A week later, Cohen and Harnick (1980, p. 204) asked the subjects a set of multiple choice questions where one of the foils was consistent with previous suggestions (for example, "Which of the following was the young woman carrying when she got on the bus? (a) an umbrella; (b) a shopping bag; (c) a newspaper; (d) a hatbox"). The findings were similar to those from the previous week: nine-year-olds were significantly more likely to remember the suggested information. The authors concluded:

> Although young children may not possess as reliable memories for real-life events as adults, they are still potentially good sources of eyewitness information. The onus is on the legal machinery to use interrogation procedures, both in the courtroom and outside, sufficiently sensitive to elicit it with minimal distortion. (Cohen and Harnick 1980, p. 209)

Stephen Ceci and his associates (Ceci, Ross, and Toglin 1987b; also discussed in Ceci, Ross, and Toglia 1987a and Toglia, Ceci, and Ross 1987) conducted four experiments designed to determine if children are "especially" suggestible compared to adults or older children. In the first experiment, children aged three to four, five to six, seven to nine, and ten to twelve were read a story with pictures about a girl's first day at school (the girl ate her eggs too fast and got a stomachache, but felt better after her friend let her play with an electronic game).

On the following day, the children were given biased or unbiased information regarding what happened in the story. Three days after the reading of the story, the subjects were asked to select which two of four pictures had appeared in the story: two pictures had appeared (a girl eating eggs and the girl with a stomachache) and two had only been suggested through the biased information given on the day following the story reading (the same girl eating cereal and having a headache). The researchers found that biased information affected the youngest subjects most, though all were affected; the three- and four-year-olds answered significantly less accurately than the two oldest groups. There were, however, no significant differences between the three groups of older children. Preschoolers, this study suggests, may be most affected by postevent communication.

Of course, these findings may be based in part on the older children's knowledge that eating too fast is less likely to result in a headache, thus making the choice between at least the headache and stomachache pictures easier for them. In other words, postevent communication may be most effective with subjects who are naive or who lack a reasonable database of knowledge from which to draw appropriate inferences. Such subjects may be more likely to accept suggestions about what they witnessed due to a lack of clearly understanding what they saw.

In a second experiment, Ceci and his associates (1987a; 1987b; Toglia, Ceci, and Ross 1987), duplicated their initial experiment, but altered the age of the confederate presenting the biased information. Children (mean age = 4.6 years) were read the story about the girl eating eggs and presented with biased or unbiased information from another child (a seven-year-old boy).[14] Two days after the presentation of the information by the child confederate, the recognition test was administered. As in the first experiment, children who were given biased information were less accurate than children who were not. The subjects, however, appeared less affected by the child confederate than had their counterparts in the previous experiment who had been given biased information by adults.[15] This finding suggests that children who are questioned by other children may provide more accurate testimony.

This second experiment by Ceci and his associates (1987a; 1987b; Toglia, Ceci, and Ross 1987) is similar to an earlier experiment conducted by Myunghi Kwock and Gerald Winer (1986, p. 292). Kwock and Winer found that nine-year-old children were significantly more accurate when asked illogical forced choice questions (for example, showing a picture of a black square and asking "Is this black or a square?") by their peers than when the same questions were asked by adults.[16]

These two studies (Ceci, Ross, and Toglia 1987a, experiment 2; Kwock and Winer 1986) suggest that children may give more accurate answers to their peers than to adults. This may be particularly true when the child witness is uncertain about what happened and merely accepted the adult questioner's suggestion because the information was believed to be correct. This idea will be discussed more fully in the next chapter.

A third experiment by Ceci and his associates (1987a; 1987b; Toglia, Ceci, and Ross 1987) utilized McCloskey and Zaragoza's (1985) Control-Standard-Modified test procedure. A picture story about a boy's first airplane ride was read to preschoolers. The next day, they were exposed to biased or unbiased information from a seven-year-old confederate. Two days later, they were asked to choose between pictures depicting correct or incorrect information. The Control and Standard groups performed as in the second experiment: those presented with biased information were significantly more likely to score lower on accuracy. The Modified group (subjects presented with misinformation followed by a choice between correct pictures and incorrect pictures containing information that had *not* been suggested to them) scored significantly higher on accuracy than the Standard group (subjects presented with misinformation followed by a choice between correct pictures and incorrect pictures containing information that had been suggested to them), but significantly lower than the Control group (subjects presented with no misinformation followed by a choice between correct and incorrect pictures). This finding could suggest that it is not the children's blind acceptance of misinformation from the interviewer, but rather deterioration of the memory for the event about which they are being questioned that causes inaccurate responses.[17] Certainly, the events of the story may not have been memorable; the questions asked about the type of juice drank by the boy in the story and the color of his cap.

Another interpretation of Ceci and his associates' (Ceci, Ross, and Toglia 1987b, experiment 3) finding is that children may have answered incorrectly because they remembered that information presented to them by adults conflicted with what they thought was the correct answer. This interpretation would take into account the difference in status between the child and adult confederate. If an adult presents the misinformation, a child may believe that his or her original (and correct) choice was actually incorrect, since an "all-knowing" adult presented information in direct conflict with the child's choice. Therefore, some children may have chosen an incorrect slide, although the information contained therein was not in the original story nor suggested by the questioner, because they believed the correct slide to be wrong (based on suggestions made by the questioner that the correct choice was actually incorrect), thus making the new foil slide the lesser of two evils.

A fourth experiment by Ceci and his associates (1987a; 1987b; Toglia, Ceci, and Ross 1987) employed a story about a school carnival with twelve illustrations. The story was read to preschoolers (mean age = 3.6 years) and college students, who were exposed to biased or unbiased information from a seven-year-old confederate on the following day.[18] Due to the adults answering "at or near ceiling in all conditions" (Ceci, Ross, and Toglia 1987b, p. 46), they were excluded from the analyses, so that the reported results applied to the preschool subjects only. The authors acknowledged in retrospect that a more complex story could have been used to prevent the ceiling effect for the adult subjects, but that such changes may have rendered the story inappropriate for the preschoolers.

As in the third experiment, children who were not given misinformation performed significantly better than those who were misled. For children who were given misinformation, those for whom the incorrect choice contained the misinformation performed significantly poorer than those for whom the incorrect choice did not contain the misinformation. In other words, the Control group (no misinformation presented) was the most accurate. The Modified group (those whose incorrect choice did not include the misinformation [for example, suggest blue cap, then present choice between correct red cap and incorrect green cap]) was second most accurate. The Standard group (those whose incorrect choice included the misinformation [for example, suggest blue cap, then present choice between correct red cap and incorrect blue cap]) was the least accurate of the three groups.

Ceci and his associates' (1987a; 1987b; Toglia, Ceci, and Ross 1987) four experiments show that children are suggestible, but that part of this suggestibility may be due to demand characteristics of the interview process. Subjects were less likely to answer incorrectly when suggestions were presented by another child. Another important finding from the experiments, however, is that without biasing, children perform nearly as well as adults.

SUMMARY

This chapter presented research showing that suggestibility is not limited to a few unsophisticated children testifying about complex issues about which they have little understanding. In fact, adults are very suggestible and are quite easily misled into remembering things that never happened. Loftus' research demonstrates this idea quite clearly.

Early researchers of the suggestibility of children felt that youngsters were far too "dangerous" as witnesses to allow them to speak in court. More recent research has found that while children are suggestible, their suggestibility may not always exceed the levels present in adults. In fact, under some circumstances, children may make better witnesses due to their lack of experience and prejudice. Finally, we learned that some of the suggestibility found in children may be attributable to their reduced status vis à vis their adult questioners.

The next chapter discusses a number of criticisms of research on suggestibility in children, then focuses on research about whether children are suggestible regarding questions that ask whether they or others have been the victims of physical or sexual abuse. Research is then presented regarding how to increase the overall quantity of information provided by young witnesses without increasing their suggestibility. Finally, a discussion of situational sources of suggestibility is presented.

Chapter 4

Realities in the Research on Children's Suggestibility: Criticisms, Increasing Accuracy, and Situational Sources

Knowledge about children's memory is limited to the superficially controlled laboratory setting; little is known about the accuracy of children's memory outside of the laboratory (Ceci and Bronfenbrenner 1985, p. 161). But it is events that occur outside the laboratory that are of interest to courts of law. Can one accurately generalize from suggestions occurring in a laboratory under controlled situations to suggestions about actual events occurring outside the laboratory?

CRITICISM #1: THE STIMULUS MATERIALS

Research presented in this book has usually involved tasks such as watching a film, viewing a slide sequence, or listening to a story, and then later answering questions as to what happened. Answers to leading questions have been used to measure the amount of suggestibility present in the child subjects. Such tasks do not involve the youngster directly, however, and the task is seldom relevant to the child. These media "stimuli may not capture children's attention in the same way that actual events do and may not be retained as well as actual events, particularly events that are personally significant" (Goodman 1984b, p. 159).

This recognition regarding the neutrality of the tests normally used to examine effects of suggestibility in children is not new. In their 1914 article, T. H. Pear and Stanley Wyatt criticize the ever-popular picture-test:[1]

> The picture can be made very complex; it may contain a great number of items, colors, positions, etc.; it is a constant and invariable stimulus, and so can be employed many times on different classes of subjects, for purposes of comparison. Its disadvantages are equally obvious. It lacks solidity, movement, and temporal sequence–three facts which detract greatly from its value in an experiment which is intended to approach the natural conditions of ordinary life. Again, it is exceedingly difficult to present a picture to a class of subjects for a definite time, and still to keep them in ignorance that they will be required to report afterwards upon what they have seen. (Pear and Wyatt 1914, p. 389)

Gail Goodman and her colleagues (1990, p. 250) suggest that "children's 'concerns'" such as children's drives, fears, wishes, and preferences play an important role in memory. If an event is personally significant (that is, it involves one of the children's concerns), the event may be more memorable. If this is true, memories of embarrassing events (such as others seeing one's "private" parts)[2] would be more memorable than memories of stories traditionally read to children.

Direct involvement of the child in the task may affect memory ability (Goodman 1984b, p. 159). Also of importance in conducting research on children is that the tasks be similar to real-life situations, since little is known about the exact process used by children when committing an event to memory. It is quite possible that actual events and secondary media events are remembered differently (Ratner, Smith, and Dion 1986, pp. 412, 426), thereby invalidating a great part of the findings based on research involving memory for stories, slides, movies, and related media.

John Yuille (1988, p. 249) reports that Mary Ann King (1984) found differences in suggestibility for live versus filmed events. King found that accuracy of memories for the events were similar, but the children were more suggestible for questions regarding the filmed event.[3] This finding supports the suggestion by Ratner and her colleagues (1986, p. 426) that secondary and primary events are remembered differently.

It is also possible that memory for uninteresting or neutral live events differs from memory for events in which the child is personally involved or has a personal interest. Goodman (Goodman et al. 1990, pp. 256-257) reports that J. E. Ochsner and Maria Zaragoza (1988) found that the free recall of children who witnessed a staged theft was better than that of children who witnessed a neutral event.[4] The children who witnessed the theft were also less likely to select a misleading answer on a forced-choice test, and were more likely to correct the interviewer when an incorrect choice was presented. Ensuring that a study is "live" is not a panacea for the ills associated with the use of media events, although Ochsner and Zaragoza (1988) point out that the control condition for their study may be more involving than the stories and films used in most research on children's suggestibility.

Note that some reports of abuse allegedly take place in neutral situations as do other events about which children may testify, therefore indicating that researchers should not "throw out the baby with the bathwater" when considering the contexts in which their live events take place. All live events used for research purposes need not be personally involving and salient for the research to have generalizability; the limitations of the findings from noninvolving events must be recognized, however, as research in neutral situations may only generalize to testimony about neutral situations.

CRITICISM #2: THE QUESTIONS ASKED

The generalizability of suggestibility studies to the courtroom is clouded because the questions used in most studies on children's suggestibility are not abuse related and focus mainly on minor or relatively unimportant details (for example, "What color was the boy's cap?"). If a detail is not personally significant to a child, however, the child may be susceptible to suggestion due to the event being "less memorable" (Goodman 1984B, p. 160). When called upon to recall the color of a storybook boy's cap (such as in Ceci, Ross, and Toglia 1987b, experiment 3), children may tend to accept suggestions because they do not remember the detail. If a child witnesses an actual event, particularly if the child is a victim-witness, the event may likely be memorable and relevant to the child; such a child would be better prepared to resist postevent information.

This acknowledgment that questions may address either neutral or salient issues was recognized in 1914 by T.H. Pear and Stanley Wyatt. The researchers argued that questions seeking minor details are more suggestive than queries for information interesting to the child:

> The most suggestive questions are those which refer to the less important or more obscure features of the event, and especially to those suggested components which might be expected to exist. On the other hand, those questions are least suggestive which refer to the most prominent [or] uncommon . . . components of the event. (Pear and Wyatt 1914, p. 419)

Gail Goodman and her associates (Goodman, Hirschman, and Rudy 1987) attack the supposition that children are extremely susceptible to suggestibility. In their 1987 presentation at the Society for Research in Child Development Meetings, they contended:

> Beginning at least with the turn-of-the-century studies by Binet, children have gained the reputation of being easily led into making false reports of abuse. But the studies upon which this assumption is based have lacked ecological validity in a number of ways. One important way is that these studies have not included questions that would be asked in actual investigations of child abuse, such as whether the child had been hit or kissed. Rather, the questions typically asked tend to focus on minor details or acts that are likely to lack personal significance for children. (Goodman, Hirschman, and Rudy 1987, p. 1)

Indeed, Goodman and her colleagues (Goodman, Hepps, and Reed 1986, p. 172) found that children questioned three or four days after a visit to a medical clinic were significantly more accurate when answering objective questions dealing with salient as opposed to peripheral information.[5] Further, all of the children correctly answered the two abuse-related objective questions (that is, "Did she put anything in your mouth?" and "Did she hit you?").

When asked misleading questions about an interaction with a male confederate which happened nearly four years before, seven-

and ten-year-old children were significantly more accurate in answering questions related to abuse than when asked questions not related to abuse (Goodman et al. 1989, p. 15). The subjects had participated as three- and six-year-olds in a previous study, during which they interacted with a male confederate for five minutes and later answered objective and misleading questions about the interaction (for details and findings for the original study, see Goodman and Reed 1986). Distributed among the questions asked in the follow-up study were therapeutic statements such as "Are you afraid to tell?" and "I've talked to a lot of other kids now who were in the room with the man, too, and they told me everything that happened to them." Although this helped create an accusatory environment, the authors concluded:

> Our findings indicate that even after a four-year delay, children were not easily led to make false reports of abuse. Given the children's lack of memory for the actual event [only 5 out of 32 children were able to recall any portion of their participation in the first study] their suggestibility should have been high. Instead, the children were surprisingly accurate in knowing that their clothes had remained on, that they had not been spanked, that they had not been touched in a place where they didn't like it, and that they had not been instructed to keep a secret. (Goodman et al. 1989, pp. 13-14)

In a later study, Goodman and her colleagues (1990, study 1) found that bystander children[6] were significantly less suggestible when asked questions related to abuse (for example, "The [person] didn't touch you, did he?") than when asked nonabuse questions (for example, "He had a beard and mustache, right?" or "He took you to another room, didn't he?"). Since many studies involve children merely observing an event, the child subjects may be more suggestible on nonabuse questions.

CRITICISM #3: ETHICAL CONCERNS

Suggestibility in actual events of interest to courts has received little research attention due to ethical concerns for staging realistic events: "We cannot, for research purposes, actively threaten children's safety or deprive them of food or comfort" (Goodman et al. 1990, p. 251). Research must fit within ethical realms, and therefore, must involve events that, at times, are not particularly salient or memorable for the child subjects. Research on stressful real-life events is necessary, however, before we can conclude that children are more suggestible than adults. Possibly through the use of already existing stressful situations (such as the medical appointments used by Goodman, Hirschman, and Rudy 1987 or the dental visits used by Peters 1987; 1991a), answers to real-life questions may be found.

The proxy research that is currently feasible can never fully address the dynamics of an actual abuse incident, especially sexual abuse. In current memory studies, children have no reason to withhold information; most of the witnessed events tend to be fairly innocuous,[7] with no apparent reason to actively deceive the research experimenter by lying.[8] As noted by Goodman, Aman, and Hirschman (1987, p. 20):

> In laboratory experiments, the children and adults have nothing to hide and thus, from the start, are likely to tell the experimenter all they remember. But this may not be characteristic of child abuse victims. . . . In these situations, children may be quite hesitant to talk about what happened, and may only gradually tell their "secrets."

This inopportune realization may mean that the memory research to date only helps to explain situations where children are eager to talk about what they witnessed (for example, minor auto accidents). The types of events about which children most often testify, however, are of abuse perpetrated on them by family members or other loved ones, or violence committed within the family unit and witnessed by a child who was in the wrong place at the wrong time. Neither event appears to be mundane or neutral for children. This, then, leads into a discussion of research regarding abuse.

"ABUSE" STUDIES

The major drawback of the studies with respect to children's testimony is that they deal with topics (for example, type of juice, color of cap) that are of little legal interest. In legal cases involving children as witnesses, identification and actions of individuals charged with physical or sexual abuse are of primary concern to the courts (Goodman et al. 1990, p. 250). The courts are usually interested in what happened and who participated; a child who is asked to testify in an abuse case is often asked to make an identification of the perpetrator and to tell about the perpetrator's activities with or in view of the child.

More salient to court cases are a set of studies by Gail Goodman, Jodi Hirschman, and Leslie Rudy (1987; also reported in Goodman et al. 1990, study 3). Goodman and her colleagues' primary focus is on whether false reports of abuse can be obtained through the use of suggestive questions; their studies tend to look at social interactions, but some address specific issues, such as the effects of stress on suggestibility (Goodman et al. 1990, study 3). As Goodman and her colleagues (1990, p. 258) assert: "If children are indeed as suggestible as some have claimed, then we should be able in our studies to create false reports of abuse."

The researchers (Goodman, Hirschman, and Rudy 1987; also reported in Goodman, Aman, and Hirschman 1987; also reported in Goodman et al. 1990; also reported in Goodman, Bottoms, Schwartz-Kenney, and Rudy 1991) questioned three- to six-year-old children who had received inoculations as part of their normal medical treatment (a real-life stress event). The children were queried on two occasions, once several days following the incident and then one year later. The researchers tried to get the children to make false accusations of child abuse through the use of leading questions (for example, "Did [the nurse] hit you?"), but were unable to do so. Although memory declined as time progressed, none of the children made false incriminations of child abuse.

The children were asked three other abuse-related questions ("Did she kiss you", "Did she put anything in your mouth?", and "Did she touch you any place other than your arm?"). Even after one year, all the children correctly answered that they had not been hit or kissed. Some errors of omission (omitting accurate information from one's report) were made in reference to putting anything in the child's mouth (the nurse had in fact given oral polio vaccines to some of the children). A small number of commission (adding correct information to one's report) errors were made regarding touching other than the child's arm, but these errors involved children stating that they had been touched on the wrist, other arm, or leg and therefore would not qualify as allegations of abuse. The authors realized that the absence of false reports in their study may be attributed in part to the children's failure to expect the nurse to abuse them. The authors also noted, however, that a number of accusations involve "teachers, church officials, Boy Scout leaders and baby-sitters," individuals who children also would not expect to abuse them; thus, the findings would be relevant to at least some cases (Goodman et al. 1990, p. 277).

A later experiment by the same researchers (Goodman, Hirschman, and Rudy 1987; also reported in Goodman et al. 1990, study 1; also reported in Goodman and Clarke-Stewart 1991, study 1; also reported in Rudy and Goodman 1991) found similar results: children questioned using suggestive techniques were able to resist suggestion when the questions asked about abuse. The four- and seven-year-old subjects were questioned by a staff associate about an incident in which the children took part in pairs–a child who participated in the activities with a confederate and a bystander child (matched to the participant child on age and gender), who merely watched the interaction.[9] Despite suggestions by the associate to report an inaccurate account, no participant child made commission errors in response to the misleading abuse questions and only one bystander child (age four) made a commission error.[10] Significant differences were found only on nonabuse questions (for example, "He took you to another room, didn't he?"); differences by age were not found for abuse questions (for example, "He took your clothes off, didn't he?" and "How many times did he spank you?").

RESEARCH ON "ABUSED" CHILDREN

Possibly of greatest concern to the validity of research on children's suggestibility when child abuse is suspected is the fact that no research to date has utilized children who are known to have been abused. Much of the research by Gail Goodman and her associates, for example, strives to determine if nonabused children will falsely report abuse. Researchers have failed to research the abused population; no child in any of the studies was hit, kissed, or mistreated in any way as part of the investigation. Differences between abused and nonabused populations may be far too great to allow generalization from one group to the other. While recent research in naturally occurring medical and dental visits has possibly replicated one part of abuse, stress, it has not replicated abuse's most important components: shame, guilt, fear, and a multitude of other feelings that may accompany physical and sexual abuse and hinder truthful reporting.

While research to date may help the courts determine whether nonabused children will falsely report abuse, it cannot assist in determining if a child who denies abuse has actually been victimized or if an abused child will falsely report the extent of the victimization. One goal of the criminal justice system is to locate abuse victims and remove them from possible future exploitation; due to no fault of the interested scholars, this goal remains necessarily unaddressed by most research.

One exception to this rule is an unpublished study by Stephen Ceci and his associates (Ceci et al. 1990, reported in Ceci 1991, pp. 8-9).[11] Preschoolers were questioned about what happened during their baths. Before questioning the children, however, the interviewer "conveyed to the children that it is naughty for adults to kiss them while the children's clothes are off" (Ceci 1991, p. 9). "Most" of the children reported that they had not been kissed.[12] Ceci and his associates' (1990) results seemingly mirror the repeated findings by Goodman and her colleagues: Goodman's subjects also reported that they had not been kissed by the nurse,[13] the pediatrician, the man in the trailer, the man who played tea party, the man who played arm movement games, or a host of other confederates utilized by Goodman's many studies. But the children in the Ceci et al. (1990) study *had* been kissed!

The children in the Ceci et al. bath study may not have seen themselves as being abused (nothing is mentioned in the Ceci (1991) write-up about who did the kissing; if parents did the kissing, the child may not view the act as unnatural), and therefore did not report the bathtime kiss. Ceci (Ceci 1991, p. 9) attributed the lack of accurate reports to a desire by the children to avoid embarrassment. Explanation notwithstanding, the children reported that they had not been kissed when, in actuality, they had. Children who have not been abused may be unlikely to falsely report abuse, but children who have experienced abuse may also fail to report its happening.

In a somewhat related study conducted by Goodman and her colleagues (Saywitz et al. 1991; also reported in Goodman and Clarke-Stewart 1991, study 5), it was found that 78 percent of five- and seven-year-old girls who received genital/anal examinations did not disclose genital touching when asked for a free recall of their medical visit.[14] Only when asked directly if the doctor "touched you here (with the researcher pointing to the vaginal area on a sexually detailed doll)" did the majority of girls report the touching. Of interest, the researchers found that seven-year-olds who received a genital examination recalled significantly less correct information about the visit than seven-year-olds who had not received a genital examination, while five-year-olds in both groups did not differ significantly in recall.

On the surface, Goodman's (Saywitz et al. 1991) subjects whose genitals had been touched do not differ much from her earlier subjects who had only received inoculations. Neither group of children was likely to report inappropriate touching during free recall; but, unlike her previous inoculation subjects, the children whose genitals had been touched accurately reported that information on direct questioning. Why didn't the children report the genital exam during free recall? Could it be that they forgot about the event until it was refreshed in their memory by the direct questions? Could it be that the children did not want to report the touching due to the embarrassment that could be caused by that type of disclosure? Or did the children not view the genital touching as worthy of report due to their expectations that medical exams include such actions and/or were they more preoccupied with other aspects of the exam, such as worrying about what was going to happen next or if any needles would be involved? Or was it that the children didn't want to speak ill of a respected person (the doctor)? The answers are unknown at this time (Goodman did not probe the children for possible answers to these questions); what is known is that the children were touched and did not report this on free recall.[15]

CHANGING CHILDREN'S INTERPRETATIONS
THROUGH SUGGESTIONS

Some of the most interesting research on children's suggestibility has been conducted by Alison Clarke-Stewart, Bill Thompson, and their colleagues (Clarke-Stewart, Thompson, and Lepore 1989; Thompson et al. 1991). These studies examined five- and six-year-olds' responses when questioned suggestively about a live event witnessed by the children. The child was left alone in an observation room for several minutes while the interviewer ostensibly left to go get more games. A confederate acting as a janitor entered the room, emptied the trash, dusted the room, and then either played with or cleaned the toys in the room. The janitor's actions were clarified by his words as each task was completed. For example, in the cleaning scenario, the janitor approached a doll and said the doll was dirty and needed to be cleaned, while in the play scenario, he said he liked to play with dolls and spray them in the face. After completing the scripted scenario, the janitor left and the interviewer returned to complete the testing. Later, a second interviewer entered the room, purporting to be the "boss of the study" who needed to know what the janitor did while in the room. In some instances, the "boss" tried to get the child to inaccurately report what had happened with regard to the janitor; varying levels of persuasion were used depending on the willingness of the child to accept the suggestions. In other instances, the "boss" simply asked the child what happened, with no suggestions offered.

Following the "boss's" questions, the original interviewer returned to the room and further questioned the child. In instances where the child had been asked to describe what happened, the interviewer simply reiterated the same sequence of questions. In those instances where attempts were made to persuade the child to report the incident inaccurately, the interviewer, through a set of leading questions, tried to get the child to report truthfully what had happened.[16] Afterwards, the child was debriefed, and then was free to leave with his or her parents.

The Clarke-Stewart et al. studies found that children questioned suggestively were significantly more likely to incorporate the interviewers' suggestions into both free recalls and direct questions regarding the event. Children questioned without the use of suggestions were accurate in their free recall and answers to direct questions:

> In the neutral [nonsuggestive] condition, children were quite accurate; that is, those who saw the janitor play gave more playing responses than those who saw him clean. By contrast, children in the suggestive interrogations appear to have adopted the suggestion. (Thompson et al. 1991, p. 9)

The accuracy of the children on a series of factual questions, however, was not effected by the suggestions. Instead, the children's answers appeared to be consistent with what they witnessed:

> The interrogations did not affect children's recollection of the 'facts' of [the janitor's] behavior; their answers to the 17 factual questions, either immediately or after a week's time, were just as accurate as those of children who heard neutral or consistent interrogations. (Clarke-Stewart et al. 1989, p. 6)

Clarke-Stewart and her colleagues (Thompson et al. 1991, p. 11) report similar findings for the 1991 study: the children's rate of error for the factual questions was not "influenced by suggestion."[17]

In a more recent study, Michelle Leichtman and Stephen Ceci (1995) focused on the effects of negative stereotypes on children's reporting about the actions by a hypothetical klutz. The authors included four conditions in their research: *control* (no stereotypes or suggestions), *stereotype* (received stereotypes only), *suggestion* (received suggestions only), and *stereotype plus suggestion* (received both treatments). Every week for a month, the preschoolers in the stereotype conditions were told a new story about the man, Sam Stone, in which he was portrayed as a "kind, well-meaning, but very clumsy and bumbling individual" (Leichtman and Ceci 1995, p. 570). Then, the children were paid a short visit by Sam Stone, during which he entered their classroom, greeted the students, walked around a bit, waved goodbye, and left. The children in the control group made the best witnesses (96 percent of their reports were accurate), and those in the stereotype plus suggestion made the poorest witnesses (64 percent accurate).[18]

Over the next ten weeks, the children in the suggestion conditions were interviewed suggestively about what had happened. The interviewers asked the children if they remembered Sam Stone's visit, during which he had "ripped that book" and "spilled chocolate on that teddy bear" (p. 571). When later asked if anything had happened to a book or a teddy bear during Sam Stone's visit, nearly three-fourths (72 percent) of the younger children in the stereotype plus suggestion condition said that Sam Stone had damaged one or both objects (p. 573). When asked if they "actually saw" him do the damage, the figure dropped to 44 percent. Even when "gently challenged" about their stories, a fifth (21 percent) of the children continued to state that they had seen Sam Stone tear the book and/or soil the teddy bear (p. 573).

These studies illustrate the ease with which children's interpretations and accounts can be colored by interviewers. In the Clarke-Stewart studies, however, the children were able to accurately answer factual questions about what they had witnessed. It was only their interpretations that were changed. In the Leichtman and Ceci study, on the other hand, the children eagerly labelled the innocent Sam Stone as the one who damaged two of their playthings.

Two important differences may account for the disparate findings. First, Leichtman and Ceci carefully established the stereotype of Sam Stone as clumsy well before any interaction, then reiterated this stereotype for months after his visit. The Clarke-Stewart studies were based instead on just one day's activities; the "boss" had only a few minutes to establish the stereotype of the janitor as "bad." In fact, the children in Leichtman and Ceci's *suggestion* condition alone were significantly more accurate than those who were exposed to both suggestion and stereotyping.

Second, is the age of the subjects. All of Clarke-Stewart's subjects were at least five years old, whereas more than half (twenty-nine versus twenty-two) of Leichtman and Ceci's subjects who were exposed to stereotypes and suggestions were younger children. Indeed, when Leichtman and Ceci categorized their results by age, they found that the older children were less than half as likely as their younger counterparts to agree that they saw Sam Stone damage the toys (p. 573).

RESEARCH SHOWING NO EFFECTS
OF POSTEVENT INFORMATION

Although postevent suggestions have been found to distort memory, this distortion need not occur (Ceci, Ross, and Toglia 1987b, p. 47). Of interest to the legal community is the finding by Ratner and her colleagues (1986, p. 426) that verbal rehearsals of events do not affect children's reporting accuracy. Children who frequently discussed at home an event to which they were exposed[19] did not perform better than children who did not discuss the event at home. Further, children who were interviewed twice did not report more after cued questioning than those interviewed only once. These findings suggest that additional in-home discussion of nonabuse events does not affect the ability of children to remember the specific details accurately. This finding, however, may only generalize to in-home discussion that is not suggestive.

INCREASING REPORT ACCURACY WITHOUT
INCREASING SUGGESTIBILITY

Since the court's objective in allowing a child to testify is to obtain the most accurate account, some researchers have attempted to learn ways to question children that do not involve the use of leading questions. Through use of such procedures, it is hoped that suggestibility will be minimized, while accuracy is maximized.

Helen Dent and Geoffrey Stephenson (1979, experiment 2) report that repeated questioning using free recall over time serves to allow children to retain the level of accuracy present during the first report, and yet, the technique does not diminish the accuracy of later recall. The ten- and eleven-year-old children were shown a "short, exciting" color film about the theft of a parcel from a car. The children were then asked for a free recall at up to five points in time: directly following the film, the day after the film, two days after the film, two weeks later, and two months later. One group of children was asked for recall at all five points in time, the second group was asked only at the two-week and two-month points, and the third was asked only at the two-month point. Those children asked for recall at all five points in time were statistically more accurate than those questioned only two weeks or two months later. Of major importance, this increase in accuracy was not accompanied by an increase in the number of incorrect points mentioned. The same study found that extended waiting periods between the event and questioning did not affect the number of commission errors, but the number of omission errors increased. This serves to increase the proportion of incorrect material in the report, however, as fewer facts are remembered after extended waiting periods.[20]

John Yuille (1988, p. 252) and Gary Melton (1981, p. 82) report that a child interviewed in a nonsuggestive manner is as capable as an adult at giving accurate testimony. Although preschoolers may provide fewer details, the accuracy of those details will not suffer as a result of the age of the witness (Yuille 1988, p. 252). There are techniques for increasing a child's recall without suggesting answers to the child. The use of anatomically detailed dolls, picture drawing, or story telling are a few indirect means by which an interviewer may learn about sexual abuse incidents. Young children are often reluctant to tell a stranger or interviewer what has happened (Faller 1984, p. 477), necessitating indirect approaches to questioning if leading questions are to be avoided. Kathleen Faller (1984, p. 478) argues that interviewers must link the scenarios containing sexual themes in play, story telling, or pictures to actual occurrences (for example, Faller asked a child who had drawn a penis on a picture of her father what a penis is, what it does, and when the child had seen it) and to allowing spontaneous recall from the child. Mary DeYoung (1986, p. 553) suggests looking for themes that exceed the psychosexual level of the child in drawings, words, and play with anatomically detailed dolls.

David Raskin and John Yuille (1989, pp. 193-194), on the other hand, argue that dolls should not be used due to lack of standardized procedures for presentation and due to the suggestibility inherent in their nature. Children notice the difference between ordinary dolls and anatomically detailed dolls almost immediately. On many anatomically detailed dolls, the genitalia are oversized to facilitate thematic play and, for this reason, may attract children's attention. And, even when presented proportionally, normal household dolls do not have pubic hair and genitalia.

Significant differences in interaction with the dolls between children referred for sexual abuse and children not referred for child abuse have been found (White et al. 1986, p. 528). These differences included more sexual themes in play/discussion for the referred children compared to no unusual behavior for the nonreferred children (this latter finding alone indicates that exposing the dolls to nonabused children need not necessarily tend to elicit reports of abuse).

In further support of the use of dolls in questioning, Gail Goodman and Christine Aman (1990, p. 1862; also reported in Goodman et al. 1990, study 2) had three- and five-year-olds play games, such as "tea party," with a male confederate. Questioning of the children one week later using sexually detailed dolls, regular dolls, or no dolls found that accuracy of free recall increased for the five-year-olds when either anatomically detailed or regular dolls were present (Goodman et al. 1990, p. 269). No differences were found between the three groups of children (no doll, regular doll, anatomically detailed doll) when the children were asked misleading questions dealing with abuse. During free recall, none of the children, regardless of the presence or absence of dolls, recalled sexualized acts. Although children questioned with anatomically detailed dolls were significantly more likely than those questioned with regular dolls to exhibit sexually related behaviors with the dolls (genital manipulation of dolls, putting the dolls in bed or intercourse), the authors concluded:

> Overall, our findings support the view that anatomically detailed dolls do not in and of themselves lead "nonabused"[21] children to make false reports of sexual abuse. . . . children did not provide spontaneous reports of sexual abuse in free recall, despite the presence of anatomically detailed dolls. Finally, children demonstrated little in the way of sexually related behaviors except to manipulate the dolls' genitalia. (Goodman and Aman 1990, pp. 1867-1868)

A second study by Goodman and her colleagues (Saywitz et al. 1991; also reported in Goodman and Clarke-Stewart 1991, study 5; also reported in Goodman and Schwartz-Kenney 1992, experiment 2) that used dolls to aid in questioning of children found complex results. Girls, aged five and seven, were asked if a doctor touched their genitals during a genital/anal examination. Free recall by the girls resulted in fewer than one-fourth of the girls reporting the touching. When dolls were introduced and direct questions asked, however, more than 85 percent correctly reported the genital contact. Girls who had a scoliosis exam substituted for the genital/anal examination consistently reported during free recall that no genital touching had occurred; when the dolls and direct questions were used, however, three of the thirty-six girls answered affirmatively, with one girl falsely stating that "the doctor used a long stick" and "it tickled" when he touched her anal area (Saywitz et al. 1991, p. 687).[22] Goodman concludes: "The data suggest that leading questions may at times be important in obtaining accurate information about genital touch from children. At the same time, there is some danger of obtaining a false report" (Goodman and Schwartz-Kenney 1992, p. 25).

It is possible that for anatomically detailed dolls to be of the most use to the courts in determining what a child witnessed or experienced, specific questions should not be employed until we find a way to minimize the likelihood of false reports as vivid as that provided by the girl who falsely claimed the doctor used a stick to touch her rectum.

The false reporting of abuse found by researchers is a topic that deserves special mention. At present, science is woefully unable to explain the bizarre reporting behavior of the girl discussed above, the boy who falsely reported that he and another boy had been spanked (Rudy and Goodman 1991, p. 533), or the boy who claimed that a research confederate used a "magic wand" to make another boy disappear (Rudy and Goodman 1991, p. 535). Indeed, researchers need to recognize the need to understand why children make false reports in addition to whether or not they are likely to make truthful ones (Meyer and Geis 1994, pp. 210-211).

SITUATIONAL SOURCES OF SUGGESTIBILITY

Some sources of suggestibility are situational, or related to the experiment at hand, rather than being related to the child's memory or ability to discriminate between imagination and reality. These "external" sources of suggestibility are not generated from within the child and, instead, usually center on the interviewers themselves.

Subconscious Messages

The awareness that questioners may include subconscious messages into their interviews is not new to science; the double-blind experiment[23] was designed to prevent such a situation, but double-blind interviewing is not a reality. Robert Buckhout (1974, pp. 28-29) reports that when Harvard's Robert Rosenthal "dropped hints" to his assistants as to the correct photograph to select from a set of faces, the results were found to support Rosenthal's opinion after the assistants administered the task. The irony of this finding is that Rosenthal had no actual theory; there was no correct photograph to select! He had only hinted at which photograph should be chosen by the subjects; his assistants must have subconsciously incorporated hints into their administration of the task. This illustrates the subliminal cues to which the subjects must have somehow been exposed during the research.

Interviewers in legal proceedings may also subconsciously guide the children they are questioning. These cues may direct the child's testimony. If the interviewer has a preconceived idea as to what happened, which is not unusual, the child may read the interviewer's cues and answer accordingly. The interviewer may also unknowingly lead the child to believe that only certain types of reports are acceptable by dwelling on certain incidents and ignoring other incidents which may be of importance to the child, but not the court (Toglia, Ceci, and Ross 1987, p. 8). How many parents have been frustrated by their children's reluctance to discuss anything other than the animals they saw at a nearby house when the parents wish to know what happened at an event that took place there?

Tone of the Interview Session

Interviewers, including therapists and other clinicians, usually begin each session with an attempt to build rapport. Reinforcement of good performance (defined here as answering questions when asked to, without reference to what those answers are) and friendliness are considered important when dealing with children. When interviewers in the legal system spend "too much" time building rapport, however, defense attorneys and other critics of children's ability to accurately testify about what they have witnessed cite this as a source of suggestibility. (This was one reason for the ultimate reversal on appeal of the conviction of Kelly Michaels, who was discussed in the first chapter.) Gail Goodman and her associates have tackled this theme (1990, study 4; also reported in Goodman and Clarke-Stewart 1991, study 3). They compared the memory and suggestibility of three- to seven-year-old children interviewed in a "reinforcement condition" (a friendly interviewer who complimented the child regularly and offered cookies and juice to the child) versus a "no-reinforcement condition" (a less friendly interviewer who did not compliment the child or offer a treat).

As part of the session, which asked questions about a visit to a medical clinic two or four weeks before, the interviewer asked suggestive abuse-related questions (for example, "She touched your bottom, didn't she?"). For the older children (aged five to seven), the interview condition did not affect the accuracy with which the children answered suggestive questions about abuse. For the younger children (aged three and four), however, those in the reinforcement condition made significantly fewer errors than those in the no-reinforcement condition when asked leading questions. The performances of the younger and older children were nearly identical in the reinforcement condition, indicating that the reinforcement condition "brought the younger children's performance up" (Goodman et al. 1990, p. 278). While this finding demonstrates that friendly interviewers may be more effective than less cordial questioners, it may only apply to cases in which children are interviewed in a friendly manner and state that they were *not* abused.[24] Future research could help us better understand the effects of session tone on the accuracy of children's recall. As demonstrated by Kelly Michaels' successful appeal, however, the courts may view zealous attempts to comfort children as unacceptable.

Wording of Questions Posed to the Child

Young children do not have as much control over language as adults. This may lead to problems during questioning when names that children have associated with items are changed by adult interviewers (Goodman 1984b, p. 164). A child may know an object by one name only and not recognize any other references to the same object; Goodman (1984b, pp. 157-158), for example, discusses a sexual abuse case where a three-year-old said he hadn't been to the suspect's house because he did not recognize that houses and apartments are viewed similarly by adults.[25] This communication gap could cause problems during an interview in which a child refers to an object by a different name than an adult, diminishing the child's already tenuous credibility with denials about situations involving the adult's terminology. Goodman and her associates (1990, study 2), for example, found that several three-year-olds and a few five-year-olds had erroneously reported that a male confederate had touched their private parts in one of their abuse studies; later questioning of the children as to the location of their private parts yielded interesting results: "The children pointed to their ears, to their arms and to other not-so-private places" (p. 270). The researchers had assumed that children understood the question, but it became apparent that the children did not share the researchers' definition of this important concept.

Young children tend to be very literal in their answers to questions (Berliner and Barbieri 1984, p. 132). A child may not consider covering something with a blanket as equivalent to putting something under a blanket, although adults readily recognize these two actions as achieving the same end result. Lucy Berlinger and Mary Kay Barbieri (1984, p. 132) tell of a five-year-old girl's testimony about her father; the girl refused to agree to statements reflecting her actions (for example, "Did you put your mouth on his penis?") while agreeing to statements reflecting her father's actions (for example, "Did he put his penis in your mouth?"). It is clear that such behavior could easily be mistaken for confusion on behalf of the child, evidence of suggestibility or possible lies.

To minimize suggestibility when questioning children, the interviewer must take into consideration the language development of the child and the difficulty the child may have in recalling the event. Language appropriate to the child should be used to avoid crossed meanings (which could occur when the interviewer means one thing and the child perceives a different meaning). The interviewer should find out what names the child has for important objects involved in the testimony, and should use those names when referring to those objects. Above all, the interviewer should avoid leading the child in any way; if the child is having memory difficulties, props can be used to "jog" the child's memory without suggestion. If the child is unable or unwilling to talk about the incident, external techniques such as picture drawing, story telling, and play with anatomically detailed dolls may serve to open the child up to the interviewer.

Authority of the Interviewer

When questions are presented to a witness in a leading manner, the witness may not accept the suggestions unless the questioner is perceived as an authority figure (Dodd and Bradshaw 1980, pp. 700-701).[26] Suggestions may be ineffective if subjects view them as coming from biased sources, possibly because subjects may not view the sources as authorities or as knowing more than themselves.

David Dodd and Jeffrey Bradshaw (1980, p. 697) studied college-aged adults who viewed a slide sequence depicting an automobile accident. When the suggestions were attributed to a person with a vested interest in the outcome of the case (in this case, a lawyer for one of the parties involved in the accident), suggestions were significantly less likely to be accepted by the subjects. A second experiment (Dodd and Bradshaw 1980, experiment 2) exposed high school students to the same slide show then to suggestions contained in a written "transcript" of an eyewitness account of what happened. When the eyewitness account was attributed to one of the parties involved in the accident, the suggestions were significantly less likely to be accepted than if the account was attributed to an innocent bystander. These two studies demonstrate that witnesses may rank the value of accounts made by various individuals and be able to withstand suggestions that are clearly subjective.

Children, however, may not so quickly realize when a source is biased. Stories are often told to children with the hopes of achieving some end result; these stories are usually tainted with some bias and some are blatant lies. Children are often told, for example, that if they eat their vegetables, they will grow to be tall and strong or if they go outside after dark, they will be kidnapped and carried off to oblivion. These stories are certainly biased towards a parent's desire for some behavior to take place, but the child still unquestionably views the parent as an authority figure.[27]

Children view adults as authority figures and as more knowledgeable than children (Ceci, Ross, and Toglia 1987b, p. 42; Goodman 1984b, p. 161). This belief may create a master/student relationship, with the child choosing to please the adult interviewer (Melton 1981, p. 80). This relationship may be troublesome, as children incorporate subconscious cues into their testimony or try to please the adult interviewer by adding information to the report due to a belief that "more is better" (Saywitz 1987, p. 47). Indeed, when children were questioned by a seven-year-old child (not an inherent authority), they were less vulnerable to suggestion; children were not as likely to accept another child's suggestions and respond to them (Ceci, Ross, and Toglia 1987b, p. 46).

The next chapter explores the argument that suggestibility may be related to children's efforts to please adult authorities.

Chapter 5

Research on Authority: Can It Help Explain Children's Testimony?

It may well be that Stephen Ceci and his associates' (1987a; 1987b) young subjects, discussed at the end of Chapter 4, were responding to authority when they answered the suggestive questions by incorporating the suggestions with which they were presented. That is, they may have been more likely to comply with the wishes of the adult questioner because they saw the adult as an authority figure while the child questioner was not seen as someone to be obeyed. Researchers interested in children's courtroom testimony should be concerned with the issues of obedience and authority. Children, when questioned either in a courtroom or in any other situation, may be less likely to be influenced by individuals who the children fail to perceive as authorities. In this chapter, the literature on authority is discussed to see how authority may alter children's testimony.

Obedience to authority by children should be an issue of interest to the courts. Of concern is the possibility that child witnesses may react to authorities who question them rather than recount the truth. The McMartin Preschool case, for example, ended in acquittals for all suspects involved due to fears about the accuracy of the testimony given by the children. The jurors were unable to determine if the children were telling the truth or simply complying with what they perceived was wanted of them by the adult interviewers. Children who react to authority cannot be relied upon to give accurate testimony.

MILGRAM'S RESEARCH

Stanley Milgram's famous findings troubled many: two-thirds (65 percent) of those he asked to inflict electrical shocks on another person obeyed and pressed levers to administer increasingly intense shocks all the way to levels, that by reasonable standards, should have been recognized as extremely harmful (Milgram 1963, p. 376; 1974, p. 35).[1] Seventeen variations of his original experiment produced similar results. In general, the subjects did what the authority told them to, whether or not it could be viewed as seriously harming another.

Milgram invited normal adult men[2] living in the communities surrounding Yale University to participate in what he told them was a study of the effects of negative reinforcement on learning behavior (for a brief description of Milgram's eighteen experiments, see Table 5.1). The subjects entered the laboratory[3] in pairs[4] and were told the following:

> . . . we know very little about the effect of punishment on learning, because almost no truly scientific studies have been made of it in human beings.
>
> For instance, we don't know how *much* punishment is best for learning–and we don't know how much difference it makes as to who is giving the punishment, whether an adult learns best from a younger or an older person than himself–or many things of that sort.
>
> So in this study we are bringing together a number of adults of different occupations and ages. And we're asking some of them to be teachers and some of them to be learners.
>
> We want to find out just what effect different people have on each other as teachers and learners, and also what effect *punishment* will have on learning in this situation.
>
> Therefore, I'm going to ask one of you to be the teacher here tonight and the other one to be the learner.
>
> Does either of you have a preference? (Milgram 1963, p. 373)

The two subjects then participated in a draw to determine who would be the learner (a person whose task was to listen and select which of a list of four words had originally been paired with a target word), and who would be the teacher (a person who would punish the learner for each mistake). The draw, of course, was rigged: the

TABLE 5.1. Brief Description of Milgram's 18 Experiments

#	Experiment	Brief Description	Obedience Rate
1	Remote	Learner in another room; no use of vocal feedback; at 300 volts, learner pounds on the wall	65.00%
2	Voice-Feedback	Vocal feedback used; begins with a simple "Ugh" and increases in intensity to "agonized screams"	62.50%
3	Proximity	Learner in same room as teacher	40.00%
4	Touch-Proximity	Teacher has to force learner's hand onto a plate that transmits shock	30.00%
5	New Baseline	Learner tells experimenter about a heart condition; vocal feedback includes reference to this condition	65.00%
6	Change of Personnel	Use of a different team; experimenter is "milder-looking," while the learner is "rougher-looking"	50.00%
7	Experimenter Absent	After giving instructions, the experimenter leaves and gives orders by telephone	20.50%
8	Women as Subjects	Same as Experiment 5, New Baseline, except the teacher is female	65.00%
9	Enters with Prior Conditions	Learner agrees to participate on the condition that he can stop at any time	40.00%
10	Office Building, Bridgeport	Study is moved from the Yale campus to an office in Bridgeport, Connecticut	47.50%
11	Subject Chooses Shock Level	Teacher is free to select the level of shock given	2.50%
12	Learner Demands to Be Shocked	Learner demands to be shocked, but experimenter disagrees and orders that the shocks be discontinued	0.00%

TABLE 5.1 (continued)

#	Experiment	Brief Description	Obedience Rate
13	Ordinary Man Gives Orders	Experimenter leaves another man in charge while he responds to a telephone call; this man orders increasing shocks	20.00%
13A	Subject as Bystander	The man in Experiment 13 begins giving shocks when teacher refuses to continue; obedience is defined as failing to protest the man's actions	68.75%
14	Authority as Victim: An Ordinary Man Commanding	Experimenter agrees to be shocked because frightened learner refuses to continue until someone else is shocked first; learner demands that experimenter be shocked even after protests	0.00%
15	Two Authorities: Contradictory Remarks	Two experimenters are present; one demands that the learner be shocked, but the other disagrees	0.00%
16	Two Authorities, One as Victim	One of two experimenters fills the role of learner when one "subject" doesn't show up for the session	65.00%
17	Two Peers Rebel	Three teachers are employed; when the subject-teacher is ordered to give higher shocks, the other two teachers disagree with the experimenter	10.00%
18	Peer Administers Shocks	Two teachers are employed; the subject-teacher watches while the other teacher gives the shocks; obedience is defined as failing to protest the other teacher's actions	92.50%

subject was always assigned the role of teacher, while the confederate[5] assumed the role of learner. The third participant in the experiment was the experimenter, portrayed by a thirty-one-year-old high school biology teacher trained for the role.

The learner was taken to an adjoining room, strapped into a chair and attached to a simulated shock generator with thirty clearly labeled voltage levels ranging from fifteen volts to 450 volts. The levels increased by fifteen-volt increments and were also labeled from "Slight Shock" to "Danger: Severe Shock." An electrode was attached to the learner's wrist after a paste was applied "to avoid blisters and burns" (Milgram 1963, p. 373). The learner/confederate then asked if the shocks would be dangerous; the experimenter replied, "Although the shocks can be extremely painful, they cause no permanent tissue damage" (Milgram 1963, p. 374). To further authenticate the experiment, each teacher was given a sample forty-five-volt shock before the experiment began.

The teacher then administered the learning task, which consisted of remembering standard word-pairs. When the learner made a mistake, the teacher was instructed to shock him. With each mistake, the voltage was increased by fifteen volts. If the subject (teacher) was unwilling to continue, a set of four prods was employed. These prods were used as often as necessary to coax the subject into continuing. The four prods follow:

Prod 1: Please continue. *or* Please go on.
Prod 2: The experiment requires that you continue.
Prod 3: It is absolutely essential that you continue.
Prod 4: You have no other choice, you *must* go on. (Milgram 1963, p. 374)

Milgram's concept of the subject's obedience was defined simply as the level at which the subject refused to administer any more shocks, despite the use of the four prods.

Milgram's findings are enlightening. If normal adult men (and women) could be induced to administer "painful" shocks to another person simply through being ordered to by an authority, how would they react to requests to do less offensive tasks, such as recounting facts from a witnessed event inaccurately? Just as Milgram utilized his four prods to obtain obedience in his experiments, so do adult interviewers of children when they ask, "Are you sure?" or repeat questions, possibly indicating that the first answer was somehow less than adequate. Therefore, the courts should have an interest in research on obedience to authority. It may be that children (and older witnesses) supply incorrect answers in order to please authorities.

For Milgram, obedience to authority involved giving shocks to another person when ordered to do so. For the courts, obedience to authority may result in inaccurate testimony when an interviewer suggests that a witness do so. The interviewer does not have to specifically order the child to lie; children may either perceive that their interviewers want certain answers or the children may perceive that the interviewers know more than they do and incorporate cues from the adults into their answers in an indirect act of obedience. Children may also assume that since one adult (the perpetrator) knows what happened, other adults, too, must know (Toglia et al. 1992, p. 227; Bull 1992, p. 9). Compliance in this case may not be obedience in the Weberian sense, that is, obedience simply due to the command issued by an authority (Weber 1947, p. 327). It is possible that children are unsure about what happened and therefore put faith in the interviewer as to knowledge of what happened. It is also possible that some children's confidence in their own opinions is very low in the first place, so that those questioned without suggestions answer accurately only because no competing explanation is offered. Indeed, those individuals who are less confident in their opinions are easier to influence to conform (Kiesler and Kiesler 1969, p. 90). Problems may also arise if a child becomes confused by the change in communication style used with adults; the rule that "adults know and children ask questions is reversed in the witness interview" (Bull 1992, p. 9). All of these possibilities help the adult take on the appearance of an authority to the child. Obedience to authority, then, may be a problem for the courts.

REPLICATIONS OF MILGRAM'S EXPERIMENTS

Several replications of Milgram's experiments have been conducted at research sites around the world. David Mantell (1971, p. 106) used males from West Germany and found results very similar to Milgram's. For his baseline condition (most similar to Milgram's original experiment), 85 percent of the subjects obeyed and pressed all thirty levers. For his control group (the subjects were told they were free to decide whether or not and at what level to shock, but if they chose to shock, the shocks should increase with each trial), only 7 percent of the subjects obeyed.

Mantell (1971, p. 104) also included a condition similar to Milgram's Experiment 17: Two Peers Rebel. In Mantell's version, the subject was scheduled to arrive early and witnessed another subject (actually another confederate) giving some shocks to a learner. The learner responded with screams of pain and requests to be released, to which the teacher/confederate responded by refusing to continue. The experimenter allowed the teacher/confederate to discontinue and then began the experiment anew with the actual subject. Fifty-two percent of the subjects in this condition obeyed.

Mitri Shanab and Khawla Yahya (1978) replicated Milgram's experiment in Jordan using male and female college students, and also found results similar to Milgram's. Nearly two-thirds of the subjects obeyed and administered the maximum level of shock—"extremely dangerous" (Shanab and Yahya 1978, p. 268). Only 12.5 percent of the control group obeyed.[6]

These replications show that Milgram's earlier findings may be generalizable to a larger population than his sample of American men. Mantell's (1971) West German and Shanab and Yahya's (1978) Jordanian subjects were just as likely to administer "painful" shocks to another person when asked to do so by an authority.

The replications may also indicate that the more control subjects have over the shock levels given, the lower their levels of obedience. Milgram's (1974, pp. 60-61) control group was directed to give whatever shock they chose, with no qualifications regarding whether or not to increase the shocks when the learner made a mistake; only 2 percent were fully obedient (fully obedient was defined as administering the highest level of shock). Mantell's (1971) control group was free to decide whether or not and at what level to shock, but if they chose to shock, the shocks *should* increase with each trial; 7 percent of the subjects were fully obedient. Shanab and Yayha's (1978, p. 268) control group was free to decide whether or not to give shocks, but if they chose to shock, each succeeding shock *had* to be one step higher than the preceding one; 12.5 percent were fully obedient. For the experimental groups, which were given no freedom to decide whether or not to shock, the percentage of fully obedient subjects jumped to 65 percent and higher. As perceived control over the process decreased, the percent of fully obedient subjects increased. This is true even within the three control groups; in studies where their actions were more constrained, the subjects were more likely to cooperate and shock the learner.

VARIATIONS ON MILGRAM'S ORIGINAL EXPERIMENTS

There have been several variations of Milgram's original experiments, each applying the overall paradigm to a different set of tasks. Researchers have spent a great deal of time designing new ways to test the various tenets of Milgram's ideas. Important knowledge can be learned from each. Six different versions are discussed below.

Variation 1: Competency Level of the Experimenter

If the authority making demands appears to be competent, obedience may be easier to secure than if the authority lacks competency. It is possible that a certain level of competency must be assumed by the subject in order for obedience to be sincere. Sincere obedience to authority does not include obedience achieved through force, such as obedience at gunpoint. This second phenomenon, coerced obedience, is not the subject of this book. The competency level of the authority in coerced obedience would not be as important in determining whether obedience takes place.

Louis Penner and his associates (Penner et al. 1973) examined the effect of their experimenters' perceived level of competency on subjects' levels of obedience. Penner and his associates invited female college students in groups of four into a laboratory to participate in a study of "physiological and psychological reactions to a particular stress situation, specifically, the shocking of a laboratory animal" (Penner et al. 1973, p. 242). The competency of the experimenter was manipulated during the study: he was portrayed as either competent (e.g., behaving in an "efficient, self-assured manner" [p. 242]) or incompetent (e.g., late, unprepared, and unable to get the equipment to work properly).

Penner's (1973, p. 242) subjects were told they would act as "harmers" (i.e., those who administered shocks to the rat) or "savers" (i.e., those who saved the rat from shocks). A subject's designation as harmer or saver alternated between trials; subjects were notified of their designation on a given trial by lights on a display panel within their sight. The rat was housed within view of the subjects in a cage with clear plastic sides. The subjects were told that whoever pressed her button first determined the rat's fate for each trial. If a harmer was fastest, the rat was shocked; if a saver was fastest, however, the rat avoided shock for that trial. In reality, however, the subjects played no role in the shocking of the rat; the rat was shocked by the experimenter "on 30 percent of the trials with a mild (.5mA) scrambled shock . . . this level of shock reliably produced results from the rat" (Penner et al. 1973, p. 242). The subjects were told they were harmers on half of the trials, and savers on the other half.

Obedience was defined simply as the "degree of adherence to the instruction to respond as rapidly as possible on *both* saving and harming trials" (Penner et al. 1973, p. 242). This formula conveniently took into consideration that some subjects were slower at responding to either designation. Smaller differences in reaction times between trials in which the subject was harmer versus saver were the sign of more obedient subjects.

Penner and his associates (1973, p. 243) found that the experimenter's perceived level of competency significantly impacted the subjects' willingness to acquiesce to his instructions to continue participating in the study. Subjects for whom an incompetent experimenter was present were less likely to press their buttons to shock the rat when designated as harmers.

Penner and his associates' (1973) research indicates that obedience may be related to the perceived competency of the authority. This would indicate that authorities who appear competent may be better able to obtain compliance than those who do not appear competent. In the courts, nearly all interviewers may appear competent, with few interviewers showing signs of inadequacy. Indeed, questions asked in the legal setting are usually framed by well-trained individuals (police officers, social workers, attorneys, judges, etc.) whose training includes the appearance of confidence, competence, and ability. Competent individuals such as these may unknowingly wrest wrongful answers from compliant children.

Variation 2: "Death" of the Victim

In addition to manipulating the competency level of the experimenter, Penner and his associates (Penner et al. 1973, p. 242) also manipulated the apparent "death" of the rat after one-half of the trials had been completed. "On the 20th trial (on which all subjects were designated as harmers), ECS was delivered along with footshock. The ECS produced convulsions and unconsciousness" (Penner et al. 1973, p. 242). After replacing the presumably dead rat with another rat, the experiment continued. The researchers (1973, p. 243) found that obedience dropped significantly after the rat's "death" for those subjects who were exposed to a competent experimenter.[7] The authors attribute this decline in obedience to the subjects' belief in the "explicit and implicit guarantees that nothing can really 'go wrong'" (Penner et al. 1973, p. 244):

> When these guarantees were attenuated . . . by the victim apparently being killed, disobedience (operationalized in this study as the difference between harming and saving RTs [response times]) increased rather dramatically. (Penner et al. 1973, p. 244)

Penner and his associates' (1973) findings indicate that once one's actions are recognized as having a negative effect (in this case, the rat's death), obedience to authority may drop. One explanation for this observed phenomenon may center on the fact that each subject, who had placed faith in the authority that everything "would work out," was shown an unpleasant side to obedience, a side which the subject may not have imagined possible given the mysterious dynamics of obedience. This realization may indicate that the authority is less competent than the subject previously imagined or that the authority is less benevolent than the subject perceived. Either way, the subject is forced to reevaluate his own and the authority's actions and wishes.

Interviewers sometimes obtain answers from young children through comforting assurances that "nothing bad will happen." Young children may be unaware of the effects of courtroom verdicts and may comply with authorities' suggestions because they believe that their testimony, as with many things they say, will be unchecked. The research by Penner and his associates does suggest this possibility.

Interviewers, however, seldom tell children the possible consequences of their testimony, typically due to attempts to appear less intimidating and to help put the child at ease when answering questions. Child witnesses are unlikely to know the unpleasant consequences of their answers to the interviewer's questions. Adults, on the other hand, may well understand the consequences of their actions for others. That this knowledge affects courtroom testimony and other behaviors is quite certain. Cesare Beccaria (1775/1983, p. 5), for example, based a large part of his mandate for lighter sentences on his belief that judges and juries failed to convict if they felt that penalties were too severe. The law codifies this knowledge by requiring a higher level of proof for criminal actions (i.e., beyond a reasonable doubt) than it does for civil actions (i.e., preponderance of the evidence).

Those children who are exposed to any negative consequences, such as the imprisonment of the alleged offender, may be told of these things in a positive light. For example, the first chapter of this book presented several interview excerpts from the Wee Care (Kelly Michaels) case; questions such as "Do you want to help us keep her in jail longer?" (Manshel 1990, p. 80) make negative consequences to the defendant seem to the child attractive or deserved.

It is possible that protecting children from the real consequences of their actions helps make inaccurate testimony reasonable given the real or perceived demands placed upon them by interviewers. If this is true, it may be useful to teach child witnesses about the legal process to help ensure that they understand their role in the system and the possible repercussions to the defendants about whom they are testifying.

Children can consider negative repercussions of their actions and base their statements upon those considerations. For example, Douglas Peters (1991a, p. 69) reports that some children in his study who failed to make correct identifications in a live lineup did not do so because of memory failure. After the identification task, they told their parents they did not identify a thief because they felt "afraid something bad might happen or that someone would get in trouble." Of course, the unfortunate presence of this adult-like tendency to avoid getting others "into trouble" would be a serious drawback to notifying children about the negative consequences that may await those against whom they are testifying.

Variation 3: Obedience as a Function of Punishment Role

Wesley Kilham and Leon Mann (1974, p. 697) extended one of Milgram's experiments (Experiment 18: A Peer Administers Shocks) to include two teachers, one who did the shocking and one who ordered the shocking.[8] Results showed that those ordering others to administer the shocks (the transmitters) were significantly more likely to obey than those giving the shocks (the executants). Fifty-four percent ordered the other teacher to give the highest level of shock, while only 28 percent of the executants delivered it when told to. None of Kilham and Mann's control subjects were fully obedient. Kilham and Mann attribute their lower figures, in part, to the national differences between their Australian sample and Milgram's American subjects, the social change that took place in the ten years following Milgram's (1963) experiments, and the modifications they made to the experiment structure.

Kilham and Mann's (1974, p. 699) findings demonstrate that subjects who perceive a direct role in harming another person may be less likely to obey than a subject whose role is less easily identified with the consequences of his or her actions. In the courts, witnesses are most similar to Kilham and Mann's transmitters. Through their testimony, they direct the courts to punish the defendant. Although this similarity is minimal at best, the allegory demonstrates how witnesses are not the actual inflictors of harm on the victim, but rather, they are purposely removed from the punishment of the defendant. This secondary role in harming alleged offenders may make inaccurate testimony more likely to occur, due to the lessened responsibility for any harm to the defendant.

Variation 4: Obedience Among Nurses

In a related study that did not use the Milgram shocking paradigm, Charles Hofling and his associates (Hofling et al. 1966, p. 174) found that 95 percent of their sample of nurses were willing to obey unfamiliar doctors' requests that a patient be given an excessive dose of an unauthorized medication. Obedience was defined as whether or not the nurse prepared the medication and started into the patient's room. The nurse was stopped from administering the medication by a second confederate.

The nurses were telephoned[9] and read the following script:

> This is Dr. Smith, from Psychiatry calling. I was asked to see Mr. Jones this morning, and I'm going to have to see him again tonight–I don't have a lot of time and I'd like him to have had some medication by the time I get to the ward. Will you please check your medicine cabinet and see if you have some Astroten? That's ASTROTEN.[10]
>
> Now will you please give Mr. Jones a stat dose of 20 milligrams–that's four capsules–of Astroten [the requested dosage, 20 milligrams, was twice the maximum dosage listed on the medication box]. I'll be up within ten minutes, and I'll sign the order then, but I'd like the drug to have started taking effect. Thank you. (Hofling et al. 1966, p. 174)

None of the nurses became hostile to the telephone caller; while 82 percent of the nurses later said they knew accepting medication requests over the telephone was a violation of hospital policy, none of them requested the order in writing. During follow-up interviews, one-half of the nurses "expressed their having had an awareness of the dosage discrepancy" (Hofling et al. 1966, p. 174).[11]

The findings by Hofling and his associates (1966) show us that nurses will accept policy-violating orders from doctors, a group to which they are institutionally subordinate. This research demonstrates how a person who not only perceives him/herself as subordinate to an authority, but also has that conception affirmed by institutional hierarchies,[12] may obey orders that could be perceived as causing great harm (possibly even death) to another person (here, the patient).

In the courtroom, interviewers of children may not only be perceived by the child as having authority, but this belief is reinforced by the child's socialization; children are taught that adults are authorities who must be obeyed,[13] thereby making children institutionally subordinate to adults.[14] When this combination of perceived authority plus institutional subordination occurs, obedience may be even more likely than in experiments using Milgram's (1963) paradigm, since Milgram's experimenter did not have institutionalized authority due to the volunteer status of his subjects.

Obedience to someone may be more likely if that person possesses institutional authority. A student in a class, for example, may be more likely than a student who was not in the class to obey his/her professor's orders. It is not the professor's lack of authority over the second student that causes this difference, it is the institutionalized subordination imposed upon the first student. While the second student simply perceives the professor as having the authority normally invested in all professors, the first student perceives the professor as having the authority invested in all professors and is institutionally subordinate to *that* professor by virtue of the school's policies. Children, on the other hand, may perceive themselves as subordinate to nearly *all* adults and, of course, to legal interviewers. Obedience, by the child witness, to the adult institutional authority may produce inaccurate testimony.

Variation 5: Refuting a Mathematical Formula

Moti Nissani (1989a, p. 22; 1989b) asked subjects to work through a self-contained instruction manual, ostensibly for the purposes of evaluating its efficiency.

At some point in the teaching process, the manual introduced a false volume formula for a sphere–a formula that led subjects to believe that spheres were 50 percent larger than they actually were. Subjects were then given an actual sphere and asked to determine its volume, first by using the formula and then by filling the sphere with water, transferring the water to a box, and directly measuring the volume of the water in the box. The key question was, would subjects believe the evidence of their senses and abandon their prior beliefs in the experimenter and the legitimacy of the entire setup? (Nissani 1990, p. 1384)

No subject definitely rejected the false formula or declined to use it in later computations. A second study (Nissani and Hoefler, in press) found similar results, although all subjects in the replication held a PhD in a natural science. Nissani (1990, p. 1385) reports that a third variation (Nissani and Maier 1990) substituted a formula regarding the circumference of an ellipse for the spherical volume formula, "thereby ruling out the possibility that earlier results were ascribed to the difficulty of dealing with three-dimensional concepts." Again, the findings were similar: ". . . all subjects clung in practice to an observationally absurd formula and none rejected it outright even on the verbal level" (Nissani 1989a, pp. 23-24).

Although Nissani's work with rejection of formulas does not seem nearly as odious as the tasks employed by some other researchers interested in obedience to authority (shocking a learner, shocking/ killing an animal, or improperly medicating a patient), the findings are nonetheless important, especially considering the 1981 ban by the American Psychological Association on research involving stress of human research subjects. Nissani's findings indicate that subjects who should know a formula is incorrect[15] will continue to use this formula until, at least, the end of the research session.

Nissani attributes the findings not to the subjects' questionable ability to "disobey malevolent authority . . . as long as the command comes from legitimate authority" (Milgram 1974, p. 89), but rather to their inability "to realize that a seemingly benevolent authority is in fact malevolent, even when they are faced with overwhelming evidence that suggests that this authority is indeed malevolent" (Nissani 1990, p. 1385). It is then, an inability "to abandon the belief in the experimenter's essential decency" that led Nissani's subjects to accept the false formula (Nissani 1990, p. 1385).

Children providing testimony may act as did Nissani's subjects. They may be unwilling to suspect court authorities of malevolence even when faced with evidence. Instead, children may answer questions to please their interviewers.

Variation 6: Inherently Dangerous Activities

In other research, Orne and Evans (1965, p. 196) found that, when asked to, research subjects would attempt to pick up a venomous snake, put their hand into a flask of acid, and throw acid into the face of another person (invisible glass protected the subject from the snake, the flask of acid was exchanged with a safe liquid at the last moment, and a second invisible glass protected the person from being splattered with the thrown acid). The subjects said they had acted as they did because they knew they would not be asked to do truly dangerous things, that the experimenter would protect them from harm (pp. 198-199). Milgram (1970, p. 141), on the other hand, cited post-experiment interviews in which 80 percent of the subjects expressed their belief that the shocks were actually being given, while less than 3 percent felt that the shocks were definitely not being given. The remaining percentage were uncertain or felt the learner "probably" was not getting shocked, despite some doubts to that belief.

Ability to fool subjects lies at the base of all obedience to authority research involving possible harm. If participants do not fall for the ruse, it is not possible to accurately measure obedience rates. Martin Orne and Charles Holland (1968, p. 287), for example, posit that Milgram's subjects (and subjects participating in similar experiments) figured out that the learner/confederate was not being harmed because the experimenter would not allow anyone to be hurt, but administered the shocks anyway to please the experimenter. This explanation may act as a confounding variable in obedience to authority research. If subjects feel the experimenter will make sure nothing unfortunate happens to them, they may also believe nothing unfortunate happens to the victim. In court, witnesses may believe that even if the interviewers are not acting in the interests of both parties, the judge will make sure that justice is served; there can be no unfavorable outcomes with a benevolent judge watching over the court. Or so think some children.

CHILDREN'S OBEDIENCE TO AUTHORITY: MILGRAM'S PARADIGM AND BEYOND

Few studies have explored Milgram's paradigm using children as subjects, although they make ideal subjects due to their unsophistication. Children do not understand the experimenter's legal obligation not to injure his subjects[16] and they seldom recognize that they are taking part in research. Since their parents consent to allow them to act as research subjects, children may not always know about their status as participants.

Research supports the view that children obey authority. Mitri Shanab and Khawla Yahya (1977, p. 533) replicated Milgram's paradigm[17] using Jordanian children aged 6-8, 10-12, and 14-16. Nearly three-fourths (73 percent) of those asked to shock the learner obeyed and administered the highest level of shock, while only 16 percent of the control subjects were fully obedient. There were no significant age or sex differences. During follow-up interviews, when the children were asked:

> to give the reason(s) for punishing the learner, they gave answers that were classified under two categories: (a) obeying orders and (b) punishment is beneficial for learning. (Shanab and Yahya 1977, pp. 533-534)[18]

The children's answers to the follow-up question are important to show that the children did not shock the learner simply because they felt the learner was not actually receiving the shocks.

A related experiment examined children's willingness to obey when their actions presented a potential danger to themselves. When asked to subject themselves to ultrasound frequencies able to produce deafness, John Martin and his colleagues (Martin et al. 1976, p. 349) found that a majority (54 percent) of thirteen- and fourteen-year-olds obeyed and turned the sound generator dial to the highest level when asked to; nearly all (95 percent) of the children subjected themselves to a sound level labeled "high danger."[19] In post-experiment interviews, 90 percent of the children said they believed the experimenter was telling the truth about the possible hearing loss, yet they did as they were asked anyway.[20]

The work of Mitri Shanab and Khawla Yahya (1977) shows us that children will obey at levels comparable (actually somewhat higher) to Milgram's earlier findings with adults. The work by John Martin and his associates (Martin et al. 1976) shows us that children will also obey even when their own safety is at stake, very similar to Orne and Evans' (1965) findings for adults.[21] Also of importance, the two experiments note that the child subjects believed the situation the researchers presented to them; the children did not behave as Orne and Evans (1965) would have predicted.

Edward Palmer (1966, p. 22) asked six- and seven-year-olds if a row of six chips had the same number of chips as a bunched group of black chips and to later determine if a short row of six chips had the same number of chips as an elongated row of six chips. Both are standard Piagetian conservation tasks. Piaget noted that a five- or six-year-old "easily constructs two sets equivalent in number, but fails to conserve the equivalence when the sets are rearranged" (Ginsburg and Opper 1969, p. 147). One of Palmer's (1966) experimental groups received a statement of surprise from the experimenter for each task on which they had been identified as non-conservers of number. For example:

> If the subject had been scored as non-conserver on the first item of the pretest, the experimenter said, "Now, remember that when we first started we had a row of black chips like this (laying out a row of black chips) and a row of red chips like this (laying out a row of red chips). You told me there was the same number of red and black chips, didn't you? Then when we did this to the black chips (bunching up the black chips), you said there were more (red, black) ones. I was very surprised when you said there were more (red, black) ones." (Palmer 1966, pp. 22-23)

Immediately following the surprise treatment, all subjects were posttested with the same two-item test used for pretesting. Results indicated that the group receiving the surprise effect made significantly greater gains in accuracy than the control subjects, who received no treatment between pretest and posttest. Although Palmer's research departs significantly from the Milgram obedience to authority paradigm, the findings are instructive.

Palmer's findings indicate that his subjects may have treated the surprise treatment as a request to change their answers to more acceptable responses. Those subjects were more likely to comply and change their answer to a correct one. It is important to note that adults readily see the fallacy in the children's answers that the numbers were unequal in number, a five- or six-year-old, however, does not see things that way. One must adopt the point of view of the child here; the child does not think to himself, "Oh, I see what I did wrong here, I simply mistakenly thought the rows were different." Rather, the child would view the rows as different and the experimenter's remarks as unexpected. Palmer's findings reinforce our belief that children view adults as authorities knowing more than the child.

Palmer's findings also show us that children's answers to questions can be changed through a simple expression of surprise. When an interviewer acts surprised at children's answers, asks "Are you sure?" or repeats a question, the children may be likely to comply with what they believe is desired and change their answers accordingly; hopefully, of course, this is not the interviewer's intention. When interviewers in court act surprised, child witnesses may alter their answers to reflect not what they have seen, but rather, to react to the interviewer's style of questioning.

CHILDREN'S OBEDIENCE TO AUTHORITY

Children generally obey authority. They are taught to respect and obey adults in most situations, even when they would choose not to. Although polling research has found that parents say they desire independence rather than strict obedience in their children (Alwin 1988, p. 42), children continue to learn through parental regulation that adults are authorities who should be respected (Milgram 1974, pp. 135-136). Parents have the task of serving as the main regulators of their children's social behavior, including children's respect for authority:

> It is the parent who first introduces the child to the laws and logic of social order. In addition to informing children about sanctions within and beyond the family, this means enforcing these sanctions and communicating to the child their social purpose.
> But introducing children to the social order means more than just getting them to obey certain rules. It also means inculcating in children an abiding respect for the social order itself. . . . Roles and responsibilities must be distributed and members of the social system must cooperate to accept their own allotted positions. This means that authority must be assumed by some individuals and deferred to by others. (Damon 1988, pp. 51-52)

There is some evidence that social class affects the value parents assign to obedience in their children. Gary Peterson and David Peters (1985, p. 81) examined differences between socialization values of low-income and middle-class mothers.[22] They found that low-income mothers valued obedience and conformity in their children significantly more so than did middle-class mothers; further, values such as the child's happiness were ranked as less desirable among low-income mothers, while ranked highly by middle-class mothers. This finding indicates, that for low-income families, greater parental emphasis may be placed upon obedience.

When the child becomes old enough to attend school, this new social institution gives the child an abundance of reasons favoring obedience to authority. While in school, children repeatedly learn that defiance is punished and obedience is "the only appropriate and comfortable response to authority" (Milgram 1974, p. 137). Indeed, Ken Rigby (1987, p. 446) found that children (mean age = 12) favorably viewed pleasing adults and teachers.[23] This phenomenon may be present in the courtroom and lead children to view satisfying adults as an attractive action.

OTHER FACTORS RELATED TO OBEDIENCE

Perceived authority status is an important variable in deciding compliance; Brad Bushman (1984) found that compliance increases significantly as perceived authority increases. Bushman's (1984, p. 503) subjects were approached by a research confederate who pointed at the experimenter (who was standing by a car parked by an expired meter) and said, "This fellow is overparked at the meter but doesn't have any change. Give him a dime!" If the subject did not comply immediately, the confederate added that he had no change either. Results indicate that as the authority level of the confederate increased (the confederate dressed as a bum, business executive, or firefighter), so did compliance to his request (p. 506). Bushman's finding may generalize to the courtroom; since perceived authority for the players in legal settings is generally quite high, obedience may be all the more likely.

In a related study, Robert Geffner and Madeleine Gross (1984, p. 978) found that obedience was greater when the experimenter's authority was increased by his wearing a uniform.[24] People about to cross a street were approached by an experimenter who said:

"Excuse me; I'm sorry but you can't cross here for a while. We've just begun to conduct some research on noise levels and uninterrupted traffic flow. You must use the crosswalk . . ." at this point, the experimenter filled in the designated location. (Geffner and Gross 1984, p. 977)

The researchers also found that obedience was significantly higher for subjects classified as younger than thirty years old when compared to subjects classified as more than fifty years old. A significant interaction indicated that younger subjects tended to obey male experimenters, while older subjects tended to disobey them.[25] The authors note that this finding may be due, in part, to the ages of the college student experimenters; their "youthfulness may have identified the experimenters as 'inappropriate' authorities to older subjects" (Geffner and Gross 1984, p. 982).

Bushman's (1984) and Geffner and Gross' (1984) finding that compliance increases as perceived authority increases indicates that if a child views an adult as an authority, compliance will be more easily obtained than otherwise. This may also be true in the justice system, especially for questions asked by uniformed police or robed judges. Geffner and Gross's finding regarding the disobedience by older subjects who may not have viewed the experimenter as an "appropriate" authority alerts us to the possibility that authority may not be guaranteed simply by possessing the title and uniform of an authority.

Adults, however, are easily identified as authorities by children, who are often forced to rely on titles and dress styles to determine power status. In this regard, Milgram notes that the "modern industrial world forces individuals to submit to impersonal authorities, so that responses are made to abstract rank, indicated by insignia, uniform, or title" (Milgram 1974, p. 137). Compounding this situation is parental stress on children's use of titles in communications with adults. Even friends of the family, for example, are often introduced to children as "Mr. X" rather than using a less formal first name or nickname. Therefore, many nonauthority adults are invested with authority by children. It is not necessary for an individual to actually be an authority to induce compliance, only that the individual be viewed as an authority by the child.

SUMMARY

This chapter presented research on obedience to authority and used it to help explain children's testimony in legal situations. Indeed, children may react to the authority vested by them in adult interviewers and may accept suggestions in acquiescence to what they feel the interviewer wishes. Other characteristics of legal interviews may also serve to enhance a child's likelihood of obedience to authority, especially the perceived level of competence and the presence of external cues of authority such as uniforms, judicial robes, or even suits, briefcases, and notebooks.

The next chapter discusses in detail Milgram's theory about why his subjects obeyed and shocked the learner. Particular attention is paid to the elements of the theory that may explain children's behavior when testifying in court. Other theories, including that formulated by Lawrence Kohlberg to explain children's levels of morality, are also presented as appropriate.

Chapter 6

Why People Obey:
Milgram's Theory

Why did Milgram's subjects obey and shock the learner? Or, less specifically, why do people obey authorities even when the orders involve harm to another person? This question is considered by John Sabini and Maury Silver:

> Suppose Milgram's experimenter held a gun to the subjects' heads; what would we expect them to do? Surely we would not be surprised if subjects obeyed then . . . we might be willing to say they "couldn't have done otherwise." But suppose Milgram's experimenter offered them $1,000,000 for obeying. Would we be surprised then if they obeyed? We doubt it; people often give into temptation. . . . What is surprising in the Milgram experiment is that people do what they know (or ought to know) is wrong even though they have nothing to fear from disobeying and nothing to gain from obeying. (Sabini and Silver 1983, pp. 150-151)

Why subjects obey authority is an important question for the courts when considering the testimony of children. Why do children "obey" adult interviewers and give inaccurate answers? Are they compliant with the ominous interviewer who forces new opinions into their young, impressionable minds? This is possible, but doesn't quite answer the question due to its circular nature (children obey because they are obedient).

Do they obey because they don't know what they are doing is wrong? Not likely. Even young children know lying is wrong (Meyer 1991, p. 22).[1] Further, avoiding punishment is the most prominent reason reported by mothers of four-year-olds for their children not telling the truth (Stouthamer-Loeber, Postell, and Loeber 1985, as reported in Stouthamer-Loeber 1986, p. 269). Children know lying is wrong, then, and reserve it for special occasions such as self-preservation and/or avoiding negative repercussions.

Do they obey because they're forced? Not possible in the real sense, since children are seldom beaten by interviewers and forced into giving answers they know are wrong. But, in an abstract sense, this may be true. Do children perceive some sort of situational dynamics invisible to the casual adult observer of the questioning session? If this is true, how can we, as adults, understand this invisible force?

The question still remains: why do people obey authorities? This question was addressed by Milgram in his 1974 book, *Obedience to Authority*. Before getting to his explanation of why people obey authorities, Milgram first sets the stage for his theory by discussing the existence of an institutionalized hierarchical structure. This hierarchical structure came about due to the social contract entered into by early man in order to gain the benefits of society:

A tribe in which some of the members were warriors, while others took care of children and still others were hunters, had an enormous advantage over one in which no division of labor occurred. We look around at the civilizations that men have built, and realize that only directed, concerted action could have raised the pyramids, formed the societies of Greece, and lifted man from a pitiable creature struggling for survival to the technical mastery of the planet. (Milgram 1974, p. 124)

Those individuals who formed the early societies found that "clearly defining the status of each member" reduced friction among the members (Milgram 1974, p. 124). When people accept their status roles in the society, "internal harmony is ensured" (Milgram 1974, p. 124). Thus, obedience to authority is inherent to the formation of societies:

Indeed, the idea of a simple instinct for obedience is not what is now proposed. Rather, we are born with a *potential* for obedience, which then interacts with the influence of society to produce the obedient man. (Milgram 1974, p. 125)

The hierarchical structure consists of a "boss" with his "followers," who may also have followers. This structure is repeated until all members of a society are followers, bosses, or both. Notice that, in such a structure, most bosses have bosses of their own, and that many followers have followers of their own; a member of a society can be both a boss and a follower. A member can follow many bosses. A quick example illustrates this concept: a child is follower to his parents and his teachers. The parents (and teachers, too) are followers to their employers, the government, their own parents, and a host of other "bosses." Children, of course, are usually always followers and are seldom bosses, except in their own hierarchies involving peers and younger siblings.[2]

When individuals obey their bosses, or, in Milgram's terminology, "enter a condition of hierarchical control, the mechanism which ordinarily regulates individual impulses is suppressed and ceded to the higher-level component" (Milgram 1974, p. 131). Thus, individuals no longer control their own behavior, the higher-level component (boss) does:

> This . . . corresponds precisely to the central dilemma of our experiment: how is it that a person who is usually decent and courteous acts with severity against another person within the experiment? He does so because conscience, which regulates impulsive aggressive action, is per force diminished at the point of entering hierarchical structure. (Milgram 1974, p. 132)

Milgram later discusses the central concept to his theory of obedience: agentic shift. Agentic shift is defined by Milgram as:

> an alteration of attitude . . . the person entering an authority system no longer views himself as acting out of his own purposes, but rather comes to see himself as an agent for executing the wishes of another person. (Milgram 1974, p. 133)

The agentic state is not "just another word for obedience . . . it is that state of mental organization which enhances the likelihood of obedience" (Milgram 1974, p. 148). When an individual feels he or she is in a situation that falls under the control of another person's authority, he or she has entered the agentic state (Milgram 1974, p. 134). The agentic state, as defined by Milgram, is in direct opposition to the concept of autonomy, or freedom to act as an independent individual. Milgram states that not all persons are destined to enter this agentic state, but "the propensity to do so is exceedingly strong" (Milgram 1974, p. 134).

Milgram's (1974) theory may also generalize to situations far less odious than the task of administering shocks to innocent victims;[3] situations such as a child's inaccurate answers during testimony may also be explained, if only in part, by Milgram's theory. For this reason, Milgram's application of his theory to his experiments is presented.

MILGRAM'S APPLICATION OF HIS THEORY
TO HIS EXPERIMENTS

Milgram (1974, p. 135) identifies three key points when applying his theory to his experiments:

First, under what conditions will a person move from an autonomous to an agentic state (antecedent conditions)? Second, once the shift has occurred, what behavioral and psychological properties of the person are altered (consequences)? And third, what keeps a person in the agentic state (binding factors)? Here, a distinction is made between the conditions that produce entry into a state and those that maintain it.

Antecedent Conditions for the Agentic Shift

When discussing antecedent conditions, Milgram mentions the familial and school influence on the developing child to obey authority. Other antecedent conditions include the existence of a "reward structure" that rewards conformity but punishes failure to comply (Milgram 1974, pp. 137-138). Good grades, job promotions, receipt of praise, etc., could all be considered rewards for compliance with authority. These forces (family, school, reward structure) act to facilitate movement into, but do not "immediately trigger movement to the agentic state" (Milgram 1974, p. 138).

These antecedent conditions are all formed during early childhood, then reinforced as necessary throughout an individual's life. Family generally continues to be a central force in an individual's life, while school is replaced at some point with the workplace and its rules and policies. The reward structure continues to exist throughout an individual's life. All these antecedent conditions can be met during the preschool years, however:

> We are taught from infancy to obey authority figures, at home and in school; taught that obedience is necessary to function in society and that it is indispensable for the existence of civilization. (Rosenbaum 1983, p. 25)

Milgram then discusses the prerequisites for entering the agentic state: (1) legitimate authority; (2) relevant authority; (3) perceived social control of the situation; and (4) legitimate ideology (1974, pp. 138-143).

Legitimate Authority

The authority figure must be perceived to have legitimate authority. For Milgram's experiments, this was achieved through several factors, including the experimenter's grey lab coat, which conveyed the concept of authority to the subject. Secondly, there was an absence of competing authorities and/or "conspicuously anomalous factors (e.g., a child of five claiming to be a scientist)" (Milgram 1974, p. 140) that would indicate to the subject that the experimenter was not an authority. These factors worked together to give the image of legitimate authority.

For children testifying in court, perception of a legitimate authority is immediate. First, children expect adults to be authorities due to their socialization regarding authority structures. Second, the adult interviewer appears to be an authority, both by dressing the part and by acting in a professional manner during the questioning. Further, if the questioning is done with parental approval, the child's parents may tell the child the interviewer is an authority.

Relevant Authority

The authority figure must be perceived as an authority relevant to the subject him/herself. Milgram notes that an individual can be perceived as an irrelevant authority, such that an individual does not define him/herself as subordinate to the particular authority (Milgram gives the example of a colonel in a parade who shouts "Left face!" not for those watching the parade, but for those marching in the parade). Milgram achieved this by conducting the experiment in the experimenter's laboratory, thereby conveying a "feeling that the experimenter 'owns' the space and that the subject must conduct himself fittingly, as if a guest in someone's home" (Milgram 1974, p. 140).

Children perceive adults to be authorities relevant to themselves for most situations. This can be illustrated by the unfortunate fact that some children will get into a car with a stranger simply by being asked to do so. Children are taught that adults are authorities and the situations during which adults are not authorities have to be explained on a case-by-case basis to the child. For example, televised media have begun to blitz children's programming with messages such as "Don't let anyone touch you where you don't want them to," and "If someone offers you drugs, it's okay to say 'No.'" These messages are needed to counterbalance the socialization of children to believe that adults are always authorities whose acts and orders are not to be questioned.

The questioning of children in legal situations involves even more relevance of authority. Children may not always understand the legal process completely, but they understand who and what police and judges are and consider them relevant authorities.

Perceived Social Control of the Situation

The authority figure must be perceived to have social control in the situation in question; that is, the subject must view the commands as appropriate to the authority figure himself. Indeed, Nicole Woolsey Biggart and Gary Hamilton (1984, p. 540) state, that in order to be powerful,[4] a person "must limit acts of power to the norms of his or her role, or convince others that he or she is exercising power within the limits of the role." Biggart and Hamilton (1984, p. 540) further state that power "actually diminishes" when the person leaves the "normative bounds" of his or her role. Milgram's commands to shock the learner do not seem inappropriate given the goals of the experiment as told to the subjects.

In a legal setting, an adult interviewer questioning a child does not ask the child to do anything inappropriate, given the situation. The only request interviewers make is that their questions are answered. Problems arise when interviewers do not always make it clear that their request is not simply for answers, but for what the child believes happened. Even here, problems may arise if a child perceives that the adult questioners merely want to confirm their own accounts of what happened or that the child's account is incorrect and must be altered.

Legitimate Ideology

The subject must view the ideology of the situation as legitimate. Subjects must not wonder why the situation is taking place; that is, there must be some explainable justification for the situation. Milgram achieved this through his statements regarding how science needs to know more about the learning process. Besides, Milgram's subjects must have felt the process of research itself was somewhat acceptable, or they would not have returned the advertisement calling for participants.

When determining if the subjects viewed the ideology of the situation as legitimate, Milgram (1972, p. 144) indicates the importance of realizing that the session began with no unjustifiable demands made of the subject. At the beginning of the experiment, there were no problems; the experiment did not begin by having the subject administer large shocks to the learner. *If* the learner made a mistake, the subject *would* shock him, but the learner had to make mistakes first. It is only later in the experiment, after the learner has made many mistakes, that the session becomes one that measures obedience to authority. By that time, however, the subject has already committed himself to participating at some level and may be unable to break the cycle of obedience. Once the task (compliance with the interviewer's wish) has been initiated, to admit at any point afterwards that one has gone too far and wishes to back out implies that a bad choice had been made to comply even in the slightest; many would rather continue to comply than make this admission (Eckman 1977, p. 97).

Turning again to children testifying in court, it is clear that under most circumstances of questioning, children have no reason to doubt the legitimacy of the situation's ideology. The justification for the situation (i.e., answering questions) is that the courts must know what the child saw or experienced. In many cases where children testify, the parents add to the legitimacy of the situation by instructing their children to answer the questions.

During the early phases of questioning, the questions may not suggest that the child change his or her answers. Most often, questioning sessions begin with some form of free recall query (for example, "What happened last night in your bedroom?"). At some point, however, the child may be unsure of the correct answer (due either to memory failure or an inability to understand the witnessed event). If children accept their interviewers' suggestions, the slippery slope is set which may not allow the children to successfully back up and change their answers. The desire to remain obedient may replace the desire to be truthful, especially if a child is unsure of what the "truth" is in a particular case. Children may differentiate between flagrant lies and falsehoods told due to ignorance of the truth. To illustrate, consider the following conversation between an interviewer and seven-year-old boy in which a child discriminates between intentional and accidental lying:

Man: What is a lie?
Boy: What isn't true, what they say that they haven't done.
Man: Guess how old I am.
Boy: 20.
Man: No, I'm 30. Was it a lie what you told me?
Boy: I didn't do it on purpose.
Man: I know, but is it a lie all the same, or not?
Boy: Yes, it is all the same, because I didn't say how old you really were.
Man: Is it a lie?
Boy: Yes, because I didn't speak the truth.
Man: Ought you be punished?
Boy: No.

Man: Was it naughty?
Boy: Not so very naughty. (Piaget 1932/1977, p. 138)

The dilemma for interviewers may intensify once the child tells the first falsehood. Children who have obeyed and told one or more non-truths may desire to avoid punishment for lying and begin to provide answers they feel will hide their earlier lies. Alternatively, the child may decide at some point that being helpful to the interviewer out-weighs any consequences due to "filling in" forgotten details.

Consequences of the Agentic Shift

Once these prerequisites have been met, movement into the agen-tic state is possible. The consequences of this movement are many. Once in the agentic state, for example, the subject himself changes:

> The person becomes something different from his former self, with new properties not easily traced to his usual personality . . . the entire set of activities carried out by the subject comes to be pervaded by his relationship to the experimenter; the subject typically wishes to perform competently and to make a good appearance before this central figure. He directs his attention to those features of the situation required for such competent perfor-mance. He attends to the instructions, concentrates on the techni-cal requirements of administering shocks, and finds himself absorbed in the narrow technical tasks at hand. Punishment of the learner shrinks to an insignificant part of the total experience, a mere glass on the complex activities of the laboratory. (Milgram 1974, p. 143)

Individuals then redefine their actions to include the authority's definition of the actions they complete (Milgram 1974, p. 145). At this point, the individuals lose a sense of responsibility for their actions; they transfer this lost responsibility to the authority. Moral-ity does not disappear altogether, but takes on a different form: feelings of shame or pride arise from the subject's perceptions of how well he has "performed the actions called for by authority." The subject's ego is not affected by the depravity of the subject's actions, but rather, his competency in executing the authority's orders.

If Milgram was able to achieve his results with an adult male sample, one would have to wonder how children, with inherently less authority than adults, would be able to effectively avoid agentic shift in their decisions to react to an authority.

Before the questioning process begins, the children are certain who the authority is; through their socialization, child witnesses know the interviewer is an authority. The relevancy of the authority is established by the goals of the questioning process itself; the child has witnessed some event in which the courts have an interest. Even if interviewers defer to children, using statements such as "I wasn't in the room, so I don't know what happened," they may not effectively dispel the children's notion of the interviewer as someone to be obeyed.

Here, the child's definition of obedience becomes paramount. If the child simply perceives that the interviewer wants to know what the child knows, problems should be minimized. If the child perceives that the interviewer wants the child to accept a different version of the account, however, the child may obey and testify inaccurately. Further, if the child perceives that the interviewer wants the truth, the child may be uncertain of what the "truth" is. If children are less than 100 percent confident about their ability to remember, they may accept cues from their interviewers as to what the "truth" is due to a belief that adults know more than children.

Once the cues have been presented through leading questions or other messages to the child (for example, repeating questions or asking "Are you sure?"), the child may compromise and accept a small portion of the cues. Ultimately, one or more questions asked during a questioning session will ask for information about which the child is uncertain, since human memory is imperfect. Once this uncertainty occurs, the child may accept cues regarding the confusing information from the interviewer.

Once any portion of the child's story is successfully changed, absorption into agentic shift becomes possible and further changes to the story may be less difficult to obtain as the child begins to incorporate more and more information from the interviewer. The child may, at some point, redefine the questioning session to be a session where the child responds to the interviewer's authority instead of the questions. This may take place without children's awareness that they are acting inappropriately, due to the redefinition of the goal of the session to include accepting incorrect information suggested by the interviewer.

Binding Factors Associated with the Agentic Shift

Once in the agentic state, the subject pales at the thought of disobeying the authority in his presence and may find compliance "less painful" than acting according to his own wishes (Milgram 1974, p. 150). Indeed, disobedience "requires overcoming the powerful habit of obeying authorities that seem to manifest itself wherever human groups are found" (Kelman and Hamilton 1989, p. 57).

One factor that keeps the subject in the agentic state is the sequential nature of the action. Milgram's subjects agreed to obey at the beginning of the experiment because they did not expect the learner to make so many mistakes requiring shocks. When the subject wants to stop participating, the experimenter simply commands him to continue doing what he has already begun. The subject is bound into the agentic state by the belief that if he stops participating at any point, "Everything I have done to this point is bad, and I now acknowledge it by breaking off" (Milgram 1974, p. 149). Furthermore, anxiety arises due to the subject's socialization towards obeying authorities, and before disobedience can be achieved, the "emotional barrier" created by this anxiety must be passed (Milgram 1974, p. 152). Taken as a whole, the move into the agentic state prevents the subject from disobeying in most circumstances. The subject is caught in a catch-22: obey and allay anxieties arising from considering disobedience (but undergo mental torment associated with violating social norms against the task) or disobey and release oneself from the torment associated with compliance (but cope with the seemingly insurmountable anxieties associated with disobedience). There are no easy alternatives for the subject once the agentic state has been entered.

When questioning children, the same sequential nature present during Milgram's experiments takes place. Questioning begins with one question and leads to others. The entire session is comprised of one question followed by another, with few breaks in the process. This helps bind children into inaccurate testimony once the first cue has been accepted. It may be difficult for children to reveal that their previous stories are not true (possibly because of perceived taboos against lying), and even if they do, this revelation could be used to claim that the children were pressured to change their stories or that at least one of their accounts is a lie.

Even if the child does not accept a suggestion, the process of suggestive questioning may continue, since the interviewer does not know what happened and is unsure of which prods are misleading.[5] After repeated presentations of incorrect information, the child can either continue to disagree or can surrender and begin to accept the adult's suggestions. This surrender may be easier if children themselves are unsure about what happened; the adult interviewer's ideas about what happened seem more acceptable to children whose own memories of the account are impaired or who are having trouble understanding the events they witnessed. According to Milgram's (1974) theory, once one suggestion is accepted, agentic shift is more likely.

In addition to the agentic shift, Milgram also accounts for compliance using other factors, including: (1) remoteness of victim; (2) ability to put the victim out of mind; (3) the fact that the subject himself is not under scrutiny by the victim; (4) lack of correlation between act and consequences for the victim; (5) exclusion of victim from group formation between authority and subject; and (6) lack of retaliation from victim (Milgram 1974, pp. 37-40). These six factors further facilitate entry into the agentic state.

These same factors pertain to children's testimony. Suspects are seldom present during the questioning of the child, satisfying remoteness of victim. (Note: The "victim" in Milgram's theory is the person who suffers due to the obedience of another. In an ironic twist, the alleged offender is now the "victim" of the child's testimony.) The child is discouraged from thinking about consequences to the suspect during questioning or is led to believe that the consequences are desirable, thus helping the child put the victim/suspect out of mind. The child is seldom under scrutiny by the suspect during the questioning, and the child may fail to see any correlation between his/her answers to questions and any negative consequences to the victim/suspect. Further, establishment of rapport between the child and interviewer does not include the suspect; the suspect is excluded from any group formation between the child and interviewer. Lastly, the lack of direct retaliation from the suspect may impact a child's ability to break out of agentic shift.[6]

AGGRESSION AS A POSSIBLE CRITICISM OF MILGRAM'S THEORY

Some of Milgram's critics have raised the possibility that innate aggression is what drove Milgram's subjects to shock the learner. Milgram denounces this argument completely, and cites Experiment 11, Subject Chooses Shock Level, as evidence supporting his position. This experiment was identical in procedure to the basic Milgram paradigm, except for one important difference: the subjects chose the shock level administered if the learner made a mistake. The experimenter told the subjects in Experiment 11 that they:

> were free to use any shock level they wished, and the experimenter took pains to legitimize the use of all levers on the board. Though given full opportunity to inflict pain on the learner, almost all subjects administered the lowest shocks on the control panel, the mean shock level being 3.6. But if destructive impulses were really pressing for release, and the subject could justify his use of high shock levels in the cause of science, why did they not make the victim suffer? (Milgram 1974, pp. 166-167)

Milgram acknowledges that some subjects behaved as they did out of aggression, but this played a small part in the outcome of the experiment:

> Now and then a subject did come along who seemed to relish the task of making the victim scream. But he was the rare exception, and clearly appeared as the queer duck among our subjects. (Milgram 1974, p. 167)

Further evidence in support of Milgram's refutation of the aggression hypothesis is found in the work of those who replicated his work and found not only similarly high levels of obedience, but also similarly low levels of obedience for their control groups (Kilham and Mann 1974; Mantel 1971; Shanab and Yahya 1977; 1978). Rather, it seems, that aggression is not the key to the explanation why Milgram's subjects were so obedient. The inaccurate testimony of children does not seem directly related to aggression at first. It is possible, however, that children may lie in order to get someone into trouble, which can be considered an act rooted in aggression. Research by Magda Stouthamer-Loeber and her associates (Stouthamer-Loeber, Postell and Loeber 1985), however, indicates that this may be untrue; children usually lie to protect themselves from punishment. Although fears of children reporting fantasy and/or lying about their experiences run amok among laypersons, these fears are unjustified. Children are not more likely than adults to tell lies (Melton 1981, p. 82), and in those cases where they do lie, they are not convincing; children are not "sophisticated liars" (Yuille 1988, p. 258). Children who make false accusations seldom have enough knowledge to appear credible before even the most believing adult after analysis of the child's remarks. Mary DeYoung (1986, p. 557) states that children coaxed into lying about sexual abuse, for example, will be unable to give specific details about the incidences in question and will not experience abuse-specific indicators.

AN ALTERNATE EXPLANATION: THE WORK OF LAWRENCE KOHLBERG

Another explanation for Milgram's findings may lie in the work of Lawrence Kohlberg, whose research focused on the moral development of children and adults. Kohlberg postulated that children have "their own morality or series of moralities" (Kohlberg 1981, p. 16). Children's moralities are not always like adults', or more specifically, the moral development of one person will differ from those who are at a different moral development stage.[7] According to Kohlberg (1981, pp. 17-19), people pass through six stages of moral development:

Stage 1.   The Punishment and Obedience Orientation–The physical consequences of action determine its goodness or badness . . . . Avoidance of punishment and unquestioning deference to power are valued in their own right.

Stage 2.   The Instrumental Relativist Orientation–Right action consists of that which instrumentally satisfies one's needs and occasionally the needs of others. . . . Reciprocity is a matter of "You scratch my back and I'll scratch yours."

Stage 3.   Good Boy-Nice Girl Orientation–Good behavior is that which pleases or helps others and is approved by them. . . .

Stage 4.   Society Maintaining Orientation–There is an orientation toward authority, fixed rules, and the maintenance of social order. Right behavior consists of . . . showing respect for authority . . . .

Stage 5.   The Social Contract Orientation–Right actions tend to be defined in terms of general individual rights and in terms of standards that have been critically examined and agreed on by the whole society. . . .

Stage 6.   The Universal Ethical Principle Orientation–Right is defined by the decision of conscience in accord with self chosen ethical principles appealing to logical comprehensiveness, universality, and consistency. . . .

Movement through Kohlberg's six stages is always "forward in sequence and does not skip steps" (Kohlberg 1981, p. 20). A person must begin at level one and proceed upwards through the other stages, one at a time. Movement into the highest stages is not guaranteed; some individuals may find themselves frozen at one stage and may not progress from there. Note that according to Kohlberg, one does not regress backwards through the stages.[8]

Kohlberg states that the stages are independent of age, and gives the example of Nazi war criminal Adolph Eichmann, a number of whose statements were scored as stage one and two. Indeed, only an estimated 5 to 10 percent of the adult population "consistently operates at stage 6" (Coon 1980, p. 440).

Classification into the stages is made based on answers to a series of moral dilemmas. An example of the moral dilemmas used for classification involves a theft in order to save a loved one's life: A man's wife is dying of cancer; to save her, he steals a drug from a pharmacist, who charges exorbitant fees for the drug. Should the man have stolen the drug? Was it right or wrong? Why? Several such dilemmas are administered and the open-ended answers are used to establish the moral development stage.

Of course, since each stage must be achieved in sequence, adults having had more time to move to higher stages during their lifetimes will generally be classified at higher stages than children, who are limited by their younger age to the lower stages. Kohlberg does not state that a child will fall into a particular stage because of his or her age. Due to its importance to the discussion of children as witnesses, however, broad estimates of the ages of individuals in each of the stages have been discussed by others (Newman and Newman 1984, p. 330) and are presented here:

- Stages 1 and 2: four to ten years of age.
- Stages 3 and 4: ten to eighteen years of age.
- Stages 5 and 6: adulthood.

Children whose testimony would be doubted in court (thirteen years of age or younger)[9] would tend to fall into the first three stages, with some "advanced" children being classified into stage four. There are great differences between those classified into each group, however, requiring a closer look at each stage in order to better understand how obedience to authority may take place.

Children[10] in Kohlberg's six stages have differing views of authority (Kohlberg 1981, p. 334). Those in stage one assign authority in relation to size, power, or visible symbols of authority. Being large, powerful, or wearing a uniform equates with authority for children in this stage. Further, a stage-one child may confuse the authority's perspective with his/her own (Kohlberg 1984, p. 174). For the courts, children in this stage could be very "dangerous" in that they would be prone to view *any* adult interviewer as being an authority worthy of obeying. To illustrate, Kohlberg gives the example of stage-one children who answered that they would "change their mind about a moral judgement for fifty cents" because "you [the experimenter] know the answer, you have the answers in the back of the book" (Kohlberg 1969, p. 441).

Children in stage two are motivated by a "desire for reward or benefit" (Kohlberg 1969, p. 381). Stage-two children present a problem to the courts when they decide to give answers because they view this behavior as resulting in a reward. This reward could be as simple as the end of the questioning session, however, pointing to the dangers of the stage-two child in the courtroom. These children would be most likely to vacillate between different versions of a story, depending on their whims at the particular moment in the questioning session. Stage-two children react to those authorities which they perceive as having some control over a given situation, such as the ability to give toys or candy or end a questioning session. Obedience for this child is viewed not so much in terms of avoiding punishment (as for the stage-one child), but rather in terms of achieving a favorable result. Interviewers who simply wish to know what happened during a given situation may find that children perceive them as authorities because of their control over the questioning session, and change their answers in response to this perception.

Stage-three children wish to meet the approval of those who are "personally worthy" (parents, teachers, and others close to the child) to them (Kohlberg 1981, p. 334). This child behaves in a way that pleases others and meets with their approval. Stage-three children become a problem for the courts when they decide that the goal of answering questions is to please their adult interviewers. The stage-three child does not view an act as "bad if it is an expression of a 'nice' or altruistic motive or person" (Kohlberg 1969, p. 380). Hence, lying in court would not be considered "bad" if the intent of the lie was to either be helpful or give interviewers the answers they seek. Consider, for example, that one of the child victim-witnesses in the Wee Care case was asked to help the interviewer "keep [the defendant] in jail longer." If this offer were posed to a stage-three child, incriminating testimony could easily result regardless of what the child actually witnessed.

Children in stage four are the most authoritarian. They position their behavior in light of fixed rules with little consideration of motives or circumstances. Stage-four children may be least likely to fall victim to obedience to authority due to their focus on relations between two individuals; these children tend to view relations as between the individual and the system (Kohlberg 1981, p. 151).

Although the stage-four child may perceive the interviewer as having authority and wanting certain answers, this child may not acquiesce to that authority due to a realization that the system itself (in this case the legal system) would not want to hear nontruths. This child feels an obligation to follow rules that are set up in the system, that is, provide truthful answers to any questions.

Kohlberg's six stages may also help explain Milgram's (1974) and other's obedience-to-authority findings. If Milgram's subjects were classified into the six stages, one may be able to predict which subjects would be more likely to question the experimenter's orders. Interestingly, Kohlberg (1969, p. 395) administered his dilemmas to a sample of Milgram's pilot subjects. He found that only one-fourth of those classified at stage six obeyed compared to seven-eighths of those classified at lower stages. It may be that Kohlberg's six stages help explain why Milgram's subjects acted as they did by showing that one's actions may be tied to one's moral development.

Kohlberg's six stages of moral development may also help determine how children will react to the authorities in their lives. If future research shows that children's moral development stages impact how they view and react to adult interviewers, this knowledge could be utilized by the courts. Prior to questioning, the child's moral development stage could be determined in order to set the tone for the questioning session. For children most likely to view any adult as an authority to be obeyed (stage one), younger/nonuniformed interviewers could be employed or interviewers could be presented to the child in a nonauthority setting. For children most likely to react to a situation according to their perceptions of rewards (stage two), interviews could be carefully structured to be short and favorable to the child; it is very important that such children do not answer according to mood and or other external stimuli. For children most likely to exhibit social desirability (stage three), the child could either be told that telling the truth (as opposed to any other answers) would please the interviewer or be asked to give answers in a way that would help prevent social desirability (for example, writing out the report or talking into a tape recorder while alone in a room). For those likely to obey institutionalized rules (stage four), the child could be educated about the rules of testifying: only answer questions for which you know the answers, do not say something untrue, and it is unacceptable to guess what happened. Remedies for the court's problems with children witnesses may, at least partially, lie in Kohlberg's six stages of moral development.

HOW CHILDREN VIEW AUTHORITY

Not all adults are viewed by children as authorities to be obeyed. Children prioritize authority as indicated by the research of Marta Laupa and Elliot Turiel (1986, p. 406), who presented children with scenarios involving a choice between which of two authorities to obey. The researchers presented first-, third-, and fifth-graders with scenarios involving turn-taking where two children (Child A and Child B) simultaneously appeared at a slide with one noninvolved individual stating that Child A should go first and a second non-involved individual stating that Child B should go first. The question posed to the child was which of the two noninvolved individuals should be obeyed.

Sometimes the noninvolved individuals were both adults, sometimes they were both children/peers, and sometimes one was an adult and the other was a child/peer. When the subjects were asked who should be heeded, they chose the recognized authority when both individuals were adults or when both individuals were peers (the recognized peer authority was a fourth- or fifth-grade trained conflict manager).

When one individual was an adult and the other was a peer, the results became more complex. As expected, when both individuals were authorities or both were nonauthorities, the adult was chosen. When the peer was an authority and the adult was not, however, the peer authority was chosen over the adult nonauthority. This interesting finding shows that children do not automatically assign authority status to all adults, but adults in positions of power are accorded respect. When both parties were authorities, the adult authority was chosen; when there was no clear authority present, the children chose the adult although the adult had no authority. When a clear peer authority was present in the absence of a similar adult authority, the nonadult/peer authority was chosen.

The researchers (Laupa and Turiel 1986, p. 408) also presented the children with a scenario involving fighting between two children. In each of three cases, an adult authority told the children to continue fighting, while a second person (either a peer authority, adult nonauthority, or peer nonauthority) told the children to stop fighting. All but one subject said the children should obey the person issuing the command to stop fighting. The authors conclude:

> The general conclusion that we can draw from these findings is that children do not take a unitary orientation toward authority. At all ages, children accepted the authority commands in some cases and rejected them in others. They accepted the legitimacy of an authority's decision in resolving the turn-taking conflict. Children also accepted the legitimacy of the command to stop fighting. However, the boundary of authority jurisdiction did not extend to commands that children continue fighting. (Laupa and Turiel 1986, p. 411)

Children, then, can make choices involving authorities; not all adults are adults who need to be obeyed. For the courts, this can be instructive. It is possible that adults can be perceived as having low levels of authority. Consider an interviewer who begins with the statement, "I don't know what happened because I wasn't there. Can you tell me what happened at school today?" This interviewer has relinquished some of his authority by "externally" dismissing it (externally in the sense that the interviewer has only changed the child's perception of him, not his ability to act efficiently as an interviewer). Since adults *can* have lower levels of perceived authority, children *can* view them as adults who do not need to be obeyed to the point of altering one's testimony.

Children usually grant adults with formal authority (teachers and other participants in the civil service field) respect with little regard for age. Conversely, at times, some individuals who possess authority may not be so perceived by children. Amiram Raviv and his associates (Raviv et al. 1990, p. 166) found that kindergartners, first-graders, and third-graders differentiated among parents, teachers, and friends when choosing epistemic authorities[11] for seven different knowledge areas (pastimes, friendships, rules and laws, personal feelings, science, future planning, and physical appearance).[12] While the kindergartners and first-graders were more likely to choose their mothers or fathers as an epistemic authority for all seven knowledge areas, third-graders were more likely to choose teachers for knowledge about science and friends for knowledge regarding pastimes. The younger children viewed their fathers as knowing more about science even though teachers have formal authority in this area. These findings may indicate that children do not automatically perceive adults (such as teachers) who are legitimate authorities as most knowledgeable in all areas of knowledge, demonstrating that children are able to assign differing amounts of authority to different adults.

Children may not automatically assume an adult with authority in one setting has authority in other settings. Marie Tisak (1986, p. 168) asked six- and eight-year-olds if parents had a "legitimate right" to expect their children to report a sibling if he stole another child's toy, did not do his chores, or played with a forbidden friend.[13]

> Children were presented with the following stories: "Let's say that the parents told _____ that they want to make a rule that if he/she sees his/her younger [sibling]: (a) take another child's toy, (b) leave his/her dishes on the table after eating, and (c) interacting with [a] forbidden friend, the older [sibling] is supposed to tell the parents. . . . What if _____ came up to you and wanted to know if you think it would be all right or not all right for his/her parents to make that rule? What would you tell him/her?" (Tisak 1986, p. 169)

Nearly all (95 percent) of the children in Tisak's (1986, p. 172) study agreed that parents have a right to expect their children to report the sibling's theft, while more than half (53 percent) of the children supported parental rules requiring them to report the sibling for not doing his chores. The children did not, however, feel that parents had the right to impose a rule which requires reporting a sibling for playing with a forbidden friend (only 27 percent felt that parents have the right to make rules about friendship choice). Tisak's findings indicate that children do not consider adults as unequivocal authorities in all cases. While children may view adults in their lives as having legitimate authority in some life spheres, this authority does not always spill over into other areas of the child's life.

Granting of "informal" authority notably decreases with age.[14] When Ann Dunbar and Beverly Taylor (1982, p. 254) asked first-, third-, and sixth-graders about their teacher's formal authority (granted to the teacher simply because of her position) and informal authority (granted to the teacher based upon her personal characteristics), grade level was found to have no significant effect on formal authority of their teachers; regardless of their age, the subjects perceived their teacher "similarly in the area of formal authority." For informal authority, however, first-graders viewed their teachers as having significantly more authority than did sixth-graders; the subjects "view[ed] the teacher's informal authority less positively as they move[d] through the elementary grades" (Dunbar and Taylor 1982, p. 254). Although the teachers never lost their formal authority, younger (versus older) children viewed their teachers as having more informal authority.

Children in the primary grades, then, may invest more "informal" authority in the adults in their life than do older children. All children may recognize that a teacher or principal (or other adult) holds a certain office and has the authority given to that office. Younger children, however, may see additional informal authority, which too, must be addressed. If this is true, obedience may be a factor of both formal and informal authority, which is exaggerated in young children because of their increased perception of informal authority.

If anything, the research on obedience to authority indicates that children are complex. Authority is not always assigned to adults, although we know little about which adults are not viewed as authorities (unfortunately, most research tends to focus on known authorities, usually parents and teachers). Peers with formal authority may be chosen over adults lacking formal authority, indicating that authority can be recognized independent of age. Children are able to assign varying amounts of authority to different adults, indicating their ability to prioritize the authorities in their lives. And finally, children may view certain adults as authorities in some situations, but not in all situations, indicating an unpredictable ability to choose to obey only under certain presently unknown circumstances. The impacts on the legal system of the research on obedience to authority are discussed in the next chapter.

Chapter 7

Conclusions and Future Directions: How Can We Bolster Children's Testimony?

Researchers agree that children and adults are, under some circumstances, suggestible. While work on suggestibility in adults has not formally moved into the public's attention, a feverish pace of work has been done with children in an attempt to discover the situations in which children are and are not suggestible. Those circumstances, at present, are very limited, however, and of little use to the courts.

Laboratory research does not always generalize to the "real world," and there is much dissension in the findings with regard to suggestibility of children. This disagreement led Stephen Ceci to write about a panel he had attended at the 1988 American Psychology-Law Society meeting:

> . . . it seemed as if one child memory researcher after another ascended the podium to report conflicting, sometimes even opposite, findings from those of his or her predecessor. (Ceci 1991, p. 1)

Children seem to be affected by authority. The research on obedience to authority indicates that people will do things they may not typically do simply because an authority asks that they do so. Due to their increased level of socialization toward respecting authority, children are more likely to find themselves in circumstances where obedience to authority is reasonable. Children, especially those confused by the legal system or what they have witnessed, may be even more susceptible to the authority of those who interview them.

All these issues cloud the testimony of children in court. For now, the courts know that sometimes children lie and sometimes they do not. More important would be the knowledge about when children will lie or the extent of the inaccuracies presented. In the interests of justice and protecting innocent defendants from undeserved punishment, the courts are forced to take a pessimistic view regarding children's testimony. For example, many prosecutors do not want to pursue cases in which a child's testimony will be weighted heavily (Berliner and Barbieri 1984, p. 127) because of the ease with which they are lost. Then, even the best prepared case must ultimately be heard by an "impartial" jury, which will usually always be instructed by the judge about the weaknesses in children's testimony.

There may be instances in which children are reliable witnesses. But we must be careful in delineating what they are. Are the situations in which children give inaccurate reports of interest to the legal system? For example, knowing that children are suggestible regarding picture books may not help the legal system determine how suggestible they are regarding whether or not someone abused them.

HOW CAN WE IMPROVE THE ACCURACY
OF CHILDREN'S TESTIMONY?

There are a number of items we can do in an attempt to improve the accuracy of children's testimony. While these suggestions cannot totally eliminate suggestibility in children, they should effectively minimize its occurrence.

Learn from Others' Mistakes

The first thing anyone who will be interviewing children in a legal setting should do is learn the pitfalls that await the children they question. One good place to start is with a careful reading of John Myers' (1987) article on techniques for direct examination, cross-examination, and impeachment of child witnesses. After a discussion about how to present one's own child witnesses in the best light (e.g., asking questions on direct examination that help establish for jurors the child's competence [p. 806], requesting periodic rest breaks so the child will not tire quickly [p. 808], refreshing children's memories during testimony [p. 815], and using expert witnesses to explain delay in reporting or presence of profile symptoms [pp. 826, 836]), Myers moves on to discrediting opposing counsel's child witnesses. His discussion is very revealing.

One approach, for example, is to trick the child into accepting a specific set of facts on the stand so as to facilitate later impeachment of the witness; earlier statements by the child can then be shown to be the product of coaching by interviewers or lying by the child (Myers 1987, p. 864). Either way, the child witness has lost a great deal of credibility. To reduce the chances of this occurring, interviewers need to refrain from providing any hint of details to the children they question. Questioning sessions should be videotaped to prevent such accusations from being levied at "overzealous" interviewers.

Myers (1987, p. 869) also recommends obtaining school records to show that the child got into trouble before the alleged incidents took place, thus casting doubt on the idea that the child is acting out due to psychological problems associated with the trauma of what was witnessed or experienced. While unrelated to actual questioning processes, this technique demonstrates how eager opposing counsel can be to discredit child witnesses.

More specifically, Myers (1987) teaches attorneys how to trick children on the witness stand. He recommends that counsel ask innocuous questions in an agreeable way before abruptly changing to substantive issues in hopes that the child will continue to agree (p. 879). Another method is to try to create false memories about unrelated incidents to depict the child as excessively suggestible (p. 887).

Attorneys can also "demolish" children's credibility by showing their propensity to engage in fantasy; Myers demonstrates this idea through showing how one boy's agreeing with counsel that he was a perfect batter was later used to undermine his other statements (p. 890). Deliberately asking questions out of order to makes it difficult for children to remain consistent in their testimony (p. 898), and anatomically correct dolls can be manipulated to make children's statements seem implausible (p. 898). When all else fails, attorneys can attack children's testimony as coached by adults (p. 894), or create anxiety in children to avoid punishment for lying about the defendant's actions as discussed below:

The . . . purpose of the questions is to induce a mild level of anxiety in the child by forcing the child to focus on punishment. Hopefully, the anxiety will combine with the fear of displeasing the attorney to strengthen the likelihood that the child will agree with counsel. (p. 881)

Understanding what children will be exposed to in court by opposing counsel should help interviewers remain professional and seek to maintain children's memories without damaging them through suggestion. Interviewers can avoid the negative lessons that others have learned. Myers (1987, p. 942) concludes his article quite clearly: "The cross examiner faces the formidable task of undermining the credibility of a child's testimony without incurring the wrath of the jury." Everyone who will interview children should commit those words to memory.

Avoid Leading Questions

Anyone who hopes to obtain an accurate account from a child (or an adult for that matter) should avoid leading questions. This is easier said than done, however, given young children's propensities to provide a bare minimum of details useful to the adults who hope to reconstruct what the child witnessed or experienced. The temptation is far too great; interviewers often wish to simply reduce the question-and-answer session to one where the child nods his head in agreement to a barrage of questions based on what the interviewer feels happened. This problem becomes all the more troublesome when the interviewer "just knows" that the child has experienced something terrible and hopes to remove the child from future danger. The use of leading questions, however, can bar effective prosecution, as learned in the McMartin and Wee Care cases. As adroitly noted by Myers, suggestibility is not the "fault" of the child witness; it is adults who "misused their authority to alter the child's recollection of events" (Myers 1987, p. 888).

Use Indirect and Nonverbal Techniques

Since we know that children react to authority, we need to do all we can to preclude them from incorporating false statements into their accounts. One obvious approach is to reduce the number of "suggestions" present in any questioning session. When children are difficult to question due to their level of verbal development, or for other reasons, interviewers can rely more on indirect techniques such as picture drawing, story telling, and play with anatomically detailed dolls, which allow interviewers to avoid leading questions. The use of models and other props also reduces the interviewer's need to communicate *to* the child, and may assist children in recalling what they witnessed. Importantly, use of these items has not been linked with increases in inaccurate testimony.

Rehearsals

We know that rehearsals or repeated free recalls may keep a child witness' memory fresh at no cost to the accuracy of their statements. It is important that the rehearsals do not involve direct questioning, and rely instead on true free recall. It may be profitable for the justice system to ask child witnesses to retell their stories on a fairly regular basis (perhaps once a week) to keep their memories strong. To reduce the chances of obedience to authority, the child could be asked by a different interviewer each time to simply retell the story. As with other questioning sessions, the rehearsals should be videotaped and parents should be instructed not to discuss the events with their children. In the end, this may help create solid memories that allow children to withstand the pressures placed on them in the witness stand by opposing counsel and accurately recount what they saw.

Reduce Perceived Authority of Interviewer

The research on authority can also help interviewers in their quest for accurate testimony. For example, such research indicates that we should try to use nonauthority interviewers or attempt to lower the chances that reports are simply the product of obedience to authority. Several ways to reduce the perceived authority of the interviewer are shown below.

Watch Question Wording

One way to reduce obedience to authority during interviews is to carefully monitor how questions posed to a child are worded. This is of paramount importance given that children are likely to vest interviewers with more authority than they deserve and may be "on the lookout" for cues. Interviewers should avoid leading questions as they may be perceived by children as hints for future answers. Unless interviewers know exactly what the child actually witnessed (which is unlikely or the child's testimony would be unnecessary), all leading questions should be avoided. When leading questions are necessary (for example, when child witnesses are reticent), interviewers should ensure that they are worded in the least suggestive manner possible. For example, using very broad-based leading questions should do less harm (e.g., "Did he touch you anywhere?" followed by "Where did he touch you?") than comparable specific questions (e.g., "Did he touch your private parts?"). Interviewers should also avoid using definite articles (e.g., 'the'), and instead rely on the use of indefinite articles (e.g., 'a') whenever feasible. Of course, interviewers should stay away from adjectives and emotional words that suggest answers or interpretations (e.g., "Did the bad man touch you here?"). Finally, questioners should avoid using words that their interviewees may not fully comprehend, due to the increased likelihood for misunderstanding. Taken together, these suggestions are a way to prevent children from garnering information about how they feel they should answer questions posed by adults in a legal setting.

Stress Interviewer's Ignorance

Another way to reduce the authority present in adult interviewers is to stress the interviewer's ignorance of what happened (e.g., state "I wasn't in the room, so I don't know what happened"). Those who interview children need to recognize that children are not accustomed to answering questions posed by adults except when they are in some form of trouble. Generally, it is the adult who holds the answers to all of life's many questions. Interviewers, then, should take extra care to convey to their young interviewees that the child is the one who has the answers, and that the adult does not know what the child saw.

Minimize Expressions of Surprise

One way interviewers unconsciously persuade children to change their stories is through various expressions of surprise.

When interviewers ask "Are you sure?", they convey to the child that the answer provided may not be the "correct" one. While adult interviewers simply use the expression to establish credibility of an answer, children may feel that its purpose is as a signal to change answers. Another subtle form of surprise involves repeating questions (as though the first answer was somehow inadequate).

Avoid Single Mind-Set Sessions

Prodding children to answer a specific set of questions when they deviate from the information being sought may reinforce their ideas about the desired track the interviewer wishes to follow. For example, children may feel the arrangement of toys in a room is very important to them although the courts seldom share this concern; by repeatedly refocusing the child on the information of interest to the courts, the interviewer may signal to the child that only certain information is appropriate to talk about. Since obedience to authority is more likely when a child feels the interviewer seeks certain answers, this scenario should be avoided. The cost, of course, is time; interviewing children can seem like an formidable task when they want to talk about mundane daily activities rather than the events they witnessed. One recommendation is to question children in rooms that are familiar to them to reduce their curiosity about the new objects in sight, or to ask questions in settings that do not involve too many distractions (especially attractive toys).

Match Questioning Style to Child's Moral Development

The questioning of children could be structured to match more closely the moral development of the child using Kohlberg's (1969) six stages of development. By classifying children before any questioning, the courts could maximize their chances of obtaining truthful testimony. And, the administration of Kohlberg's dilemmas may serve to acclimate the child to the questioning session and help build rapport between the interviewer and child.

Purposely Vary Dress and Age of Interviewers

Experiments with adults have shown that external vestiges of authority affect compliance with commands; there is no reason to suspect that children do not react similarly to known authorities. In order to reduce their perceived level of authority, those who interview children may purposely "dress down" in casual clothing and "loosen up" their demeanor in an attempt to reduce their level of prestige with child witnesses. Attempts to make the session less formal could also include leaving clipboards and notebooks out of sight, and failing to take notes (other individuals outside the room can take down answers through the use of hidden microphones and videotapes can be used to supplement notes). Reducing interviewers' status may pay off well if children do not react to authority.

Teach Children About Their Role in the Courts

One important step in improving children's performance in court is to educate them about what is expected of them. At present, there are few films and books designed to answer children's questions and address their fears about what happens in court. We should focus on developing materials to fill this essential need. One good example is the film *B.J. Learns about Federal and Tribal Court*, distributed by the Department of Justice's Office for Victims of Crime to teach American Indian children about the differences between tribal and United States federal courts and about their role in both. In addition to factual material about the courts, the film stresses the obligation of the protagonist to tell the truth. Books and workbooks could also help address this concern and demystify part of the courtroom process for young witnesses.

Training Children to Answer Questions

In order to help reverse the tendency to comply with an interviewer's subtle requests to report inaccurately, children could be exposed to a situation and then questioned about what they saw. Through this exercise, the child could be "made accustomed" to being the person with the answers to the adult's questions. In addition, such an exercise may ease the child's apprehension regarding the actual questioning session. It would be important, however, to ensure that inaccurate answers during this mock session not be used to show that the child is or is not suggestible. For one thing, we do not know if suggestibility in one situation generalizes to another. The purpose of the exercise would simply be to allow the child to give answers to questions posed by the interviewer in addition to setting up rapport between the interviewer and child.

Teach Children to Watch for Misleading Items

Myunghi Kwock and Gerald Winer (1986, p. 290) found that nine- and twelve-year-old children exposed to "flagrantly misleading" items (for example, showing a picture of couch and asking the child "Why is this a car?") were better able to resist less flagrantly misleading questions presented later. A control group of children did not receive the flagrantly misleading questions and were more likely to accept the suggestions presented on the target items. "Presumably, this effect was due to the cuing items' sensitizing the subjects to the misleading implications of the questions and, thus, to the possibility of the alternative and more accurate responses" (Kwock and Winer 1986, study 1, p. 291). Is it possible to train children to be on the lookout for misleading questions in order to help them increase their own report accuracy? Future research should explore this possibility.

DIRECTIONS FOR FUTURE RESEARCH

Future research on suggestibility should explore the dynamics of obedience through experimental manipulation of interviewers' levels of authority. For example, in the Clarke-Stewart studies (Clarke-Stewart, Thompson, and Lepore 1989; Thompson et al. 1991), the interviewer could have been a child who was announced to the subject as another youngster who had come into the room to play. In other instances, the child interviewer could be introduced as a room monitor. An adult could be introduced as the boss or an adult with no authority, such as a person looking for misplaced books. Such manipulations would allow researchers to determine to what extent authority may affect suggestibility. It is obvious that children will lie in some situations; the question is not necessarily "Will they lie?". The fact that children lie when adults suggest they should is not surprising. The true research question is what approaches are likely to obtain the most "truth" from the child, that is, what kind of mechanisms will allow us to use their statements.

Other directions of interest include the circumstances under which children will react to authority. It is possible, for example, that children react to authority only when they perceive that the authority's wishes are more appropriate than the child's own.

Of equally great interest is the question of obedience when the child is previously warned of the authority's attempt to gain compliance. Will children react less to authority if they are told the authority will try to trick them into saying something untrue? Research could help us understand this possibility.

Future research should also include baseline measures before offering suggestions to ensure that compliance can be attributed to the suggestions presented, rather than a reaction to a new authority or inability to correctly recall from memory. Many studies to date do not include a neutral questioning session before the suggestive questioning begins. This failure to establish baseline memory for an event allows for multiple explanations of the same phenomenon. It is important to determine the child's level of accuracy on free recall before beginning the suggestive questions that form the core of the research inquiry.

What is needed in the field is knowledge about *when* children will react to authority and provide an inaccurate account. It is already widely known that children (and adults) are suggestible under certain circumstances. What is not known is if children are suggestible in affairs of concern to the legal system. More research is necessary in this arena to gain better insight into the phenomenon of obedience to authority in the courtroom.

The layperson's belief that children are excessively suggestible will continue to plague the courts until viable options are found. In the meantime, however, cases involving children's testimony will continue to be dropped for "lack of evidence," although children's reports are a potential plethora of information. How do the courts get this information without changing it? This is a true catch-22: to retrieve the information may damage it, but to refuse to try is injustice.

It may be impossible to determine at all times if children are honest, just as it is impossible to determine if adults are always honest. The courts have always faced this problem, and have relied on the ability of "twelve good men" to judge a witness's veracity. Indeed, the jury's belief as to the veracity of a given witness may determine the outcome of a case. For example, although the Wee Care and McMartin cases were similar in many respects (abuse at day care center, perpetrated by staff, multiple victims, quasi-ritualistic events), the trial juries reached very different verdicts. One of many reasons for this difference lay in the testimonies of the children involved: their testimonies were perceived as credible in one case and seriously doubted in the other.

We cannot, through research, eliminate lying. We can only try to prevent lying that is the direct result of questioning practices. Reaction to authority, obviously, will change children's testimony under some circumstances. Although we cannot totally eliminate obedience to authority from children, we can try to eliminate authority as a factor in court. Through lowering the authority factor in interviewers, we may be able to increase the amount of truth in children's reports.

The courts may find it necessary to employ interviewers who are less likely to be viewed as inherent authorities by children (young, no uniforms, casually dressed, low prestige). In an attempt to lower the chances of obedience to authority, the courts may implement practices such as intentionally exposing children to events and asking them what happened to get child witnesses accustomed to answering questions in a legal setting. Educational materials such as films and books may be designed to educate child witnesses about their role in the legal system and the purpose of the questioning sessions in which they will participate. The courts may some day realize they cannot simultaneously place so much stress on child witnesses' truthfulness and the austerity of the courts, since it may be this focus on formality and seriousness that leads child witnesses to utter the nontruths so condemned by the courts. In the end, however, we will still be forced to rely on the judgements by judges and juries as to the accuracy of a given child witness' statements in court.

Notes

Chapter 1

1. According to David Finkelhor and his associates (1988, p. 8), the McMartin case "did the most to galvanize the issues and anxieties surrounding this problem [sexual abuse in day care]." One of the issues, of course, is prosecution of possible incidents of abuse.

2. It was not until January, 1986, that it became clear to those involved that the McMartin students' testimony was not strong enough to fully prosecute all seven suspects.

3. The Salem witch trials were the first United States criminal cases in which children were called upon to testify (Ceci, Ross, and Toglia 1987A, p. 79).

4. Some scholars have considered medical explanations for the witch scare, including the possibility that some of the villagers were afflicted with convulsive ergot poisoning (which results from eating contaminated grain), which could have caused its victims to hallucinate and feel as though they were being choked, pricked, and bitten by witches (Caporael 1976, p. 21)

5. Each subject's memory for the event was tested using free recall, objective questions (with one leading question), and the photo identification task. After a two-week period, each subject was asked to repeat the memory test, except that the leading question was changed to a nonleading form.

6. For two of the sequences, the thief and picnickers were adults (mean age = 24 years). For the remaining two sequences, the thief and picnickers were children (mean age = 9 years). Within each age group, two different people served as the thief. All four sequences depicted the same scenario.

7. Of interest, a "sizeable proportion of changes" were from initially correct to incorrect choice or vice versa. Not all changes reflected a move from an incorrect choice to another incorrect choice.

8. The differences between the three-year-olds and both older groups were significant (Goodman and Reed 1986).

9. The children (N = 6), who ranged from third to eighth graders, were selected from a local chess tournament. The adults were graduate students and research assistants. The chess positions were eight "middle-game positions" using approximately twenty-two pieces each chosen from a chess quiz book (Reinfeld 1945) and shown to the subjects for ten seconds. The subjects then had to completely recall the entire board, including pieces, colors, and positions.

10. Of interest, Fore (1978) asked her fifth-grade students who their favorite actor/actress was. More than a fourth (27 percent, n = 6) listed one of the actresses

from *Charlie's Angels*, thereby indicating the show's popularity with children of the time.

11. Of interest, a control list containing words from standard Battig and Montague (1969) categories showed that the college students recalled more than the nine-year-olds.

12. The finding that boys remember more details than girls appears to be fairly regular in early research on memory (see also, Dupré 1910, p. 355).

13. Subjects were tested on two occasions: immediately following the reading and five days later. The first questioning session consisted of a free recall period, cued questioning, then six direct questions about a specific character (three of which contained suggestive misleading information). During the second questioning sessions, the free recall and cued questioning were readministered, followed by a prompt to describe the character as fully as possible. The session was constructed as closely as possible to an actual questioning session by police and/or parents.

14. The research confederate was seven years old and mentioned his name and hometown at the beginning of the session, which took place one day after the reading of the story. The Ceci, Ross, and Toglia experiments are written up in detail later in this book.

15. For this study, Ratner and her colleagues tested the memory of kindergartners and college students after a structured session of making and playing with clay. After free recall had been exhausted, cuing began regarding the session. One-half of the subjects were tested both immediately after the session and one week later; the other half were not tested immediately following the session, but were tested at the one week follow-up.

16. Event-tests are explained in Whipple (1909, p. 156) as those "in which opportunity is supplied for report upon human activities under realistic conditions." Examples of suggested event-tests include attendance at the theater and use of the "moving-picture show."

Chapter 2

1. Parents rated the child's stress level during the visit using a six-point scale. The scale ranged from "extremely happy or relaxed" to "extremely nervous or upset."

2. The researchers attempted to make the treatment of each pair of children as comparable as possible. For example, if a six-year-old girl from the previous study received an oral polio vaccine and two shots in her arm, a new six-year-old girl was given a liquid candy administered by mouth and had two tattoo designs rubbed on her arm.

3. Parents, dentists, and dental assistants provided anxiety ratings (on a nine-point Likert scale) for each child during the dental visit. Later measurement of anxiety levels during the recognition session conducted at the subject's home found significantly lower stress levels than for the dental visit.

4. These findings are for the target-present lineups (lineups for which the picture of the target person is one of the choices). For the target–absent lineups (line-

ups for which none of the pictures is of the target person), there were no significant differences in accuracy between the two groups. The children were also asked to identify the voices of the dentist and dental assistant from a five-voice audiotaped lineup. There were no reliable findings for this task, however, due to difficulty for the children.

5. These findings are again for the target-absent lineups; there were no significant differences in accuracy between the two groups.

6. These findings are again for the target-present lineups. For the target-absent lineups, there was no significant difference in accuracy between the two groups.

7. This citation is interesting because the authors stress that they found "only scant evidence" linking stress and recall ability (Ornstein, Gordon, and Larus 1992, p. 58). They further state (p. 59) that their findings are closer to Goodman's (1987) findings than Peters' (1987) results.

8. With the exception of the two studies reported here.

9. In one Goodman study (Hepps 1985 as reported in Goodman, Aman, and Hirschman 1987), stressed and nonstressed children were asked to identify the individual who gave them an inoculation three or four days earlier. The two groups did not differ in their ability to make a correct identification, but other problems plagued the task; there were only nine experimental children and only one false identification was made by either group, indicating that the task may have been too simple to discriminate between the two groups. Due to these problems, the study should not be considered as supporting either Peters' or Goodman's research.

10. Since this was their first or second visit to the dentist, Peters' subjects would be unable to use memory from previous visits to help identify the correct room. Since those items normally associated with a dental visit (dental chair and instruments) were present in all the photographs, the selection task would be difficult for those children who paid little or no attention to the room.

11. Direct questions are the most common from of cued recall (Cole and Loftus 1987).

12. The confederate asked the subject several questions (e.g.: "What is your name?") and then instructed the subject to follow him in performing a series of arm movements. The subjects were told that the study was concerned with age differences in motor learning and that they would be playing a game with a man.

13. If the child had not mentioned a man in a jacket, such a question would be leading because it implies that the man wore a jacket.

14. Prices' subjects repeatedly participated in a sequence of events involving twenty-one details. Recall for five-year-old subjects' correctly recalled items dropped to about eighteen when the model was not used.

15. Saywitz (1987), for example, in her study using audiotaped stories, noted that a few of her subjects recalled information that would have taken place after the story ended, indicating that children may imagine and recall information not present in the original memory. For instance, one child stated that the character in

the story "got on a bus" after the story ended, although there was no material presented to the subjects about what happened to the character following the story.

16. The age of the witness is not mentioned in the article.

17. This was similar to the first part of the second experiment, except that the subjects were told to imagine themselves saying the word as opposed to hearing another person say it. After the session, the subjects were asked if they had said the word, imagined themselves saying the word, or if the word was a new word which had not been said or imagined.

18. There were three conditions: the subjects either (1) performed some actions and watched another person perform other actions, (2) watched two others perform actions, or (3) performed some actions and imagined themselves performing other actions. The actions fell into the category of simple movements and actions (e.g.: shake your head, touch your elbow, look at the door, do a jumping jack). After each session, the subject was asked if the action was new or (1) if they did it or someone else did, (2) which of two others did it, or (3) if they did it or imagined themselves doing it.

19. The mean number of correct responses out of twenty possible is kindergartners = 14.00; second graders = 17.35; fourth graders = 18.15; and sixth graders = 19.45. Further analysis showed that more fantasy characters were classified as real than real characters classified as fantasy. Nearly 80 percent of the mistakes by the second, fourth, and sixth graders involved classification of three "deliberately ambiguous characters" (Indian, knight, and dinosaur) as fantasy. One-half of the kindergartners' mistakes fell into this category.

Chapter 3

1. The estimates were as follows: smashed–40.8; collided–39.3; bumped–38.1; hit–34.0; and contacted–31.8.

2. In this study (Loftus 1977), college students were shown a series of thirty color slides depicting an auto-pedestrian accident and later asked twelve questions containing one target item. The target item asked if the "blue" car that drove by in the slides had a ski rack on top (the car was actually green). Subjects who were exposed to the target item were significantly more likely to respond that the car was blue.

3. More than one-half of the witnesses remembered seeing the theft.

4. For a good historical review of research on suggestibility of children, see Goodman 1984a.

5. Whipple (1912) reports that Varendonck's testimony "elicited violent outbursts from the court authorities," but succeeded in producing an acquittal. Regarding the case, Whipple (1912, p. 268) stated that the psychology of testimony had formally entered into the courtroom and "saved a man's life."

6. The interaction lasted from two minutes and ten seconds to two minutes and thirty-five seconds.

7. The researchers also examined differences between normal children and "mentally defectives," defined as "children of such a degree of mental sub-

normality that they had been adjudged to require teaching in 'special' schools" (Pear and Wyatt 1914, p. 394).

8. Although the research took place in 1939, the Ministry of Justice report is now out of print. The report cited here was written up in 1982 and contained a summary of his previous work.

9. Good factual memory for the story was indicated by answering two factual questions correctly. This second analysis was conducted "in order to analyze the answers to the follow-up questions independently of the developmental improvement in memory" (Duncan, Whitney, and Kunen 1982, p. 1218.

10. The story was the same for each group of children, but could be interpreted differently for each orientation. For example, the story mentioned that the protagonist "could hear . . . the uniformed band" chasing him; subjects who received the escaped convict orientation were significantly more likely to incorporate statements such as "prison guards were chasing him," while those who received the *Planet of the Apes* orientation were more likely to make statements such as "a monkey running away from the mean gorillas" (Brown et al. 1977, p. 1459).

11. Another classic study along these lines is the work by Gordon Allport showing that subjects were likely to state that the black man in a picture of an altercation on a subway train held a weapon when in reality, the white man held it (Buckhout 1974, p. 26).

12. Half of the questions were suggestive. Two versions of the question were used; half of the subjects were interviewed using Version 1 and the remainder were interviewed using Version 2. If a question was suggestive for one version, it was not suggestive for the other.

13. In addition, the performance of the nine-year-olds on the nonsuggestive questions was significantly lower than either twelve-year-olds or adults.

14. The authors state that efforts to train a confederate younger than seven were unsuccessful.

15. Only those subjects from the first experiment who fell into the exact age range of the second experiment (forty-two to sixty-eight months) were included in the combined data set.

16. Answering "both," "A and B," or "Yes" was considered a correct answer.

17. Ceci and his associates (1987b) indicate that this shows the merit of McCloskey and Zaragoza's (1985) argument, but does not adequately dispel the myth of the suggestible child; their subjects were still vulnerable to suggestion. In a later article, Zaragoza (1991) proposed that Ceci's findings may result from differences between the studies and then tested for the effects of each difference. Zaragoza's subjects (mean age = 4 years, 11 months) were older than Ceci's (mean age = 3 years, 8 months), but Zaragoza's later replication of the study using three-year-olds failed to show evidence of memory impairment (1991, experiment 1). When Zaragoza raised the control performance to that of Ceci's subjects through lessening the number of filler slides and lengthening the exposure time, she again failed to show evidence of memory impairment (1991, experiment 2). When Zaragoza shortened the retention interval to match that of Ceci's, she again found no evidence of memory impairment (1991, experiment 3).

18. The information regarded the color of a clown's balloons and the type of fruit eaten by the protagonists.

Chapter 4

1. The authors also criticized the neutrality of live events used by their predecessors and colleagues: "up to the present, it seems to have been comparatively simple, so that there has been relatively little to report when it was over, and hence the opportunity of studying individual differences has not been great" (Pear and Wyatt 1914, p. 389).

2. Goodman et al. (1990) note that one of the first things children are taught is to be embarrassed concerning sexuality and exposure of their bodies (Jackson 1982, pp. 100,180).

3. The recorded event was of a theft of a purse from a woman's shopping bag. For the live event, a person entered the room and talked with the child. Yuille (1988) does not discuss how King (1984) controlled for the differences in the two events.

4. The first-grade children were left in a school room to complete a puzzle when a man entered, asked for the school principal, and moved about the room. For the theft condition, he stole a purse on a table and left. For the control group, he merely left in search of the school principal.

5. The divisions into salient and peripheral information were completed by "a group of graduate students, naive to the hypotheses of the study" (Goodman, Hepps, and Reed 1986, p.171).

6. Bystander children watched while another child (matched to the bystander child in age and sex) interacted with a male confederate in a trailer. This study is discussed in more detail later, in the section titled "Abuse studies."

7. With the exception of some of the research on the effects of stress by Peters (1987; 1991) and Goodman (Goodman, Aman, and Hirschman 1987; Goodman et al. 1990; Goodman, Bottoms, Schwartz-Kenney, and Rudy 1991; Goodman, Hirschman, Hepps, and Rudy 1991).

8. With the exception of the secret condition utilized by Clarke-Stewart and her colleagues (1989) and Goodman and Schwartz-Kenney (1992) discussed elsewhere in this book.

9. The children interacted with a male confederate during a twelve-minute session that took place in a trailer. The interaction consisted of playing Simon Says, dressing the child in a clown costume which fit over the child's own clothing, taking pictures of the child, thumb-wrestling, and playing a game invented for the experiment (the game, The Funny Things Clowns Do, involved such actions as the child tickling the confederate). Ten to twelve days after the session, the children were asked to recall what happened and then asked a series of direct questions (for example, "He took your clothes off, didn't he?").

10. The child who made the commission error falsely stated that he and the participant child had been spanked (Rudy and Goodman 1991, p. 533).

11. Due to potential ethics and human subjects committee problems, this study involved the researchers' own young children (Ceci, 1992).

12. In his 1991 write-up, Ceci does not give exact statistics regarding the number of children who reported whether or not they had been kissed.

13. Several studies utilized nurses.

14. Included in the study was a Control group of girls who received a scoliosis examination in place of the genital examination. Children were examined and then questioned one week or one month later, using free recall, demonstration of the event with anatomically detailed dolls, and direct questions.

15. There was an important difference between Ceci's and Goodman's studies, however–method of questioning. Goodman's subjects were first asked for a free recall whereupon they did not report the touching. When asked directly if their genitals had been touched, Goodman's subjects did report the touching. Ceci and his colleagues' subjects were asked directly about whether or not they had been kissed while their clothes were off; the children still did not report any kissing.

16. In the 1989 study, however, the interviewer asked the "boss's" suggestive questions a second time in an attempt to get the child to report inaccurately. In other words, if the "boss" suggested that the janitor was playing instead of cleaning, the interviewer also suggested that he was playing.

17. A closer look at whether children would agree with just those false statements that were consistent with the suggestions, however, yielded a marginal ($p = .06$) effect for interrogation style (suggestive or nonsuggestive).

18. The stereotype group was 83 percent accurate, and the suggestion group was 72 percent accurate (p. 573).

19. A session with clay during which the children first made clay and then played with it.

20. If the child only remembers ten of fifty details after a time delay, for example, one commission error represents a much higher proportion of the report than if the same child remembered forty of the fifty details.

21. It is important to realize that designation as "nonabused" merely indicates that the child is not known to have been abused in the past. For any given "nonabused" child, it is possible that abuse has taken place, but has remained undetected.

22. The other two girls who falsely reported genital touching were unable to provide any details.

23. The double-blind experiment is one in which neither the subject nor experimenter knows to which group the subject has been assigned. An example of a double-blind experiment would be the administration of either actual medication or a placebo to a research subject by an experimenter who cannot tell the difference between the tablets. If the experimenter does not know to which group the subject is assigned, "this prevents them from unconsciously influencing the subject or being influenced themselves" (Coon 1980, p. 36).

24. Indeed, we sometimes forget that accurately stating that one was not abused when no abuse occurred is just as important, if not more important, than accurately disclosing abuse. We also forget that accurately denying that abuse has taken place and accurately disclosing abuse are not similar events; one has a large, emotionally charged, potentially embarrassing component.

25. The child repeatedly denied visiting the suspect's house, but agreed that he had been to his apartment and willingly told about what had happened there.

26. Authority is defined in *Webster's Dictionary for Everyday Use* (1981) as "legal power or right, accepted source of information . . . a body or group of persons in control."

27. Or at least until adolescence when children begin to question the authority and intentions of their parents. It may be that authority is sometimes misattributed to adults before the onset of adolescence.

Chapter 5

1. A "control group" of subjects (Experiment 11: Subjects Free to Choose Shock Level) who were given a choice regarding the shock voltage showed that subjects were unwilling to utilize high voltage shocks when they were not ordered to do so: only one of forty (2 percent) subjects pressed the 450-volt switch.

2. In one variation of Milgram's study (Experiment 8: Women as Subjects), women were used as subjects. In all seventeen other versions, the subjects were male.

3. In one version of the study (Experiment 10: Institutional Context), the laboratory was moved to what appeared to be a private research group, Research Associates of Bridgeport, located in Bridgeport, Connecticut. All other experiments were conducted on the Yale University campus.

4. In several versions of the experiment (for example, Experiment 15: Two Authorities: Contradictory Remarks and Experiment 17: Two Peers Rebel), the standard research format of three participants (a "learner," "teacher," and experimenter) was modified to allow for more participants.

5. The confederate was played by a forty-seven-year-old accountant, who had been trained for the role.

6. The control group here was told that they were free to choose whether shocks were given during the experiment. If they chose to shock, however, "each succeeding shock had to be one step higher than the preceding one" (Shanab and Yahya 1978, p. 268). They were, however, free to continue the experiment without giving any shock at all, by continuing the process (administering the word pairs) without punishing the learner.

7. There were no significant differences between obedience before and after the rat's "death" for the incompetent experimenter. The authors attribute this, in part, to the subjects' lack of surprise regarding the event:

"It seems reasonable to propose that subjects in the competent experimenter condition were a good deal more surprised by the killing of the rat than were the subjects in the incompetent experimenter condition. Thus, their behavior changed much more dramatically" (Penner et al. 1973, p. 244).

8. Subjects were assigned to one of two experimental conditions: one where the subject ordered a research confederate to administer the shocks, or one where the subject gave shocks as ordered by the confederate. If a subject was in the control group, "he was placed in either a transmitter or executant role, but was told he was free to choose the level of shock himself" (Kilham and Mann 1974, p. 698).

9. Accepting medication orders over the telephone was in violation of hospital policy.

10. Astroten was a placebo packaged to resemble actual medication. The box read "ASTROTEN," gave the capsule size as five milligrams, listed the usual dosage as five milligrams, and listed the "maximum daily dosage" as ten milligrams.

11. A control group of twelve graduate nurses were read the scenario and asked to respond with what they would do in such a situation. Ten (83 percent) of the graduate nurses said they would not give the medication; the remaining two nurses (17 percent) would have given the medication as directed. A second control group of twenty-one student nurses (included to determine how "less experienced" nurses would react) were also read the scenario and asked to respond; all the student nurses said they would not give the medication as requested.

12. This usage of "institutionalized hierarchies" is not to be confused with Milgram's usage of the phrase, which is discussed in the next chapter. The phrase is used here to denote hierarchies that are not only apparent to those within the hierarchy, but can be understood by those outside the hierarchy due to written or well-understood policies implemented by the organization governed by the hierarchy. For example, armed forces written policy dictates that soldiers must obey the orders of lieutenants, who must obey the orders of generals.

13. Research by Donata Fabbri Montesano and Matilde Panier Bagat indicates that children understand the concept of obedience to authority. The five- to eleven-year-old subjects were asked to complete three short stories involving obedience to another child, an adult, or a parent. They were then asked to explain and justify their responses. Responses varied according to the status of the persons to be obeyed, indicating that children as young a five "are able to appreciate the nature of the power relations in which they are involved" (1988, p. 37).

14. Parents are usually the primary vehicles by which children are socialized, but this position is shared, to a lesser degree, with child care workers (Toner 1986, p. 27).

15. It is clear that the subjects should have either known the formula from their own knowledge or noted the discrepancy when performing the comparison tasks (pouring water from the sphere into the box and measuring the contents of the box).

16. This addresses Orne and Holland's (1968) argument of subjects figuring out that no harm is being delivered to the learner. Unlike more sophisticated adults, children may not believe the experimenter will protect them from harm.

17. Milgram's (1963) paradigm is discussed earlier in this chapter.

18. Regretfully, the article does not mention the percentage of children falling into each of the two categories.

19. The subjects were told they were being tested to determine if they possessed a special ability to hear sounds which are normally beyond the range of human hearing. The potential danger involved at each level of the "ultrahigh-frequency sound emitter" was clearly displayed in a chart given to the subjects; for

example, the warning for level six (for which 95 percent of the subjects complied) read "High Danger Level- 20 percent hearing loss becoming increasingly likely."

20. Of interest, many (59 percent) of the subjects reported hearing sound through the headset attached to the sound generator although no sound was able to pass through the headset. This finding is reminiscent of Loftus' findings regarding reports of nonexistent items incorporated into adult eyewitness reports; here, it is nonexistent sound that the children reported. The question then becomes did they "hear" the sounds because they wanted to be in the select group who could hear high frequency sounds or did they "hear" the sounds they felt the experimenters wanted them to hear?

21. Of course, Orne and Evans (1965) reported that their subjects obeyed because they trusted the experimenter and did not believe he would allow any real harm to come to anyone in the experiment, while Martin and his associates (1976) found that their child subjects believed they could be harmed.

22. Low-income was not a stand-in for minority racial status; both black and white low-income mothers were included in the study.

23. The subjects (mean age = 12 years) were asked to complete the L scale measure of social desirability of the Junior Eysenck Personality Questionnaire (Eysenck and Eysenck 1975), the Teacher and Parent Subscales of the Children's Attitudes to Authority Scale (Rigby and Schofield 1985), and the Schoolchildren's Authoritarianism Scale (Ray and Jones 1983). Results showed that measures of proauthority attitudes and behaviors correlated positively with the L scale measure of social desirability.

24. The uniform identified the experimenter as an employee of the Santa Clara Valley Department of Public Works, Research Division.

25. No significant differences were found for female experimenters.

Chapter 6

1. Meyer (1991) examined the answers to two questions about lies provided by forty-three five- and six-year-olds. The first question asked for the definition of a lie and whether it is wrong to lie; all but one child knew what a lie was and felt it was wrong to lie. The second question asked if it was okay for a seven-year-old birthday girl to lie about her age to get into Disneyland for half price; again, only one child felt it was okay for the girl to lie (this child felt it was okay because it was the girl's birthday).

2. To illustrate the concept of children's hierarchies, consider Jean Piaget's observation that, while playing marbles, four- to six-year-old boys strongly "desire to play like the other boys, and especially like those older than himself" (Piaget 1932/1977, p. 36).

3. The reduced distaste associated with giving inaccurate testimony (as compared to administering shocks to another person) may be important. Kiesler and Kiesler (1969, p. 55) note that greater compliance can be expected for less offensive tasks.

4. Being powerful indicates an ability to obtain compliance.

5. The most serious problem associated with the use of leading questions is that interviewers do not know which are misleading and which are correctly leading.

6. This is not to be confused with a child's belief that the alleged offender will retaliate in response to the child's testimony at a later point in time. Here, the suspect's absence from the questioning session prevents retaliation during the session and thus, does not preclude the child from continuing to answer questions.

7. This is not meant to be circular. Kholberg felt that individuals differ from each other in their level of moral development. He then classified the stages he felt people go through and stated that persons at one stage differ in their moral development from those at other stages.

8. Kholberg demonstrated the "cultural universality" of his six stages (1984, p. 23). He queried boys from Mexico, Taiwan, Turkey, and Yucatan in addition to his original United States sample and found that his stages were valid. He also notes no "important differences" among Catholics, Protestants, Jews, Moslems, and atheists for the stages (1984, p. 25).

9. For states using them, competency tests are usually administered to children under the age of fourteen.

10. Of course, Kohlberg notes that his stages transcend childhood, but for this book, I have chosen to focus on the children in each of the stages. None of the stages has a definite age group that it covers, since peoples' moral development seems to occur somewhat independent of age.

11. Epistemic authorities are those authorities which are relied upon for knowledge. "Individuals have high confidence in the validity of information provided by epistemic authority, consider it truth, assimilate it into their own repertoire, and rely on it" (Raviv et al. 1990, p. 158). Epistemic authorities are individuals whose information is regarded as "more truthful" than that of others (Raviv et al. 1990, p. 158).

12. For each of the seven knowledge areas, the subjects were asked who their epistemic authority was (for example, the question for science read, "who knows best, in your opinion, why the sun disappears at night, or why it is cold and rains in the winter?").

13. Tisak also interviewed a sample of ten-year-olds, but these results are not discussed here.

14. The authors explain informal authority of a teacher in the following manner: ". . . the teacher must 'win' from the students the right to make and enforce decisions that will affect them; he or she must win the pupils' trust and liking and be perceived as caring and working hard for the pupils' sake" (Dunbar and Taylor 1982, p. 250).

References

Alwin, D.F. (1988). From Obedience to autonomy: Changes in traits desired in children, 1924-1978. *Public Opinion Quarterly*, 52, 33-52.

Babinsky, A. (1910). *Die Kinderaussage vor Gericht; vortrag gehalten in der vereinigung der richter in Berlin*, Berlin.

Battig, W.F. and Montague, W.E. (1969). Category norms for verbal items in 56 categories: A replication and extension of the Connecticut category norms. *Journal of Experimental Psychology Monograph*, 80, (June pt. 2), 1-46.

Beccaria, C. (1775/1983). *Dei delitti e delle pene*, (4th ed.). London: Printed for F. Newberry, 1775. Translated and reprinted (1983) as: *An Essay on Crimes and Punishments*. Brookline Village, MA: Branden Press Inc.

Berliner, L. and Barbieri, M.K. (1984). The testimony of the child victim of sexual assault. *Journal of Social Issues*, 40, 125-134.

Biggart, N.W. and Hamilton, G.G. (1984). The power of obedience. *Administrative Science Quarterly*, 29, 540-549.

Binet, A. (1897). Psychologie individuelle. La description d'un objet. *l' Année psych*, III, 296-332.

Binet, A. (1900). *La Suggestibilité*. Paris: Schleicher-Frères.

Binet, A. (1905). La science du témoignage. *l' Année psych*, XI, 128-137.

Binet, A. (1911). Le bilan de la psychologie en 1910. *Année psych*, XVII, v-xi.

Binet, A. and Henri, V. (1894). Mémoire des phrases. *l' Année psych*, I, 24-60.

Brainerd, C. and Ornstein, P. (1991). Children's memory for witnessed events: The developmental backdrop. In J. Doris (Ed.), *The Suggestibility of Children's Recollections: Implications for Eyewitness Testimony*. Washington DC: American Psychological Association.

Brown, A.L., Smiley, S.S., Day, J.D., Townsend, M.A.R., and Lawton, S.C. (1977). Intrusion of a thematic idea in children's comprehension and retention of stories. *Child Development*, 48, 1454-1466.

Buckhout, R. (1974). Eyewitness testimony. *Scientific American*, 231(12), 23-31.

Bull, R. (1992). Obtaining evidence expertly: The reliability of interviews with child witnesses. *Expert Evidence: The International Digest of Human Behavior, Science and Law*, 1, 5-12.

Burgess, A.W., Holmstrom, L.L., and McCausland, M.P. (1978). Counseling young victims and their families. In A.W. Burgess, A.N. Groth, L.L. Holmstrom and S.M. Sgroi (Eds.), *Sexual Assault of Children and Adolescents*. San Francisco: Lexington Books.

Bushman, B.J. (1984). Perceived symbols of authority and their influence on compliance. *Journal of Applied Social Psychology*, 14, 501-508.

Caporael, L.R. (1976). Ergotism: The Satan loosed in Salem? *Science*, 192, 21-26.

Ceci, S.J. (1991). Some overarching issues in the children's suggestibility debate. In J. Doris (Ed.), *The Suggestibility of Children's Recollections: Implications for Eyewitness Testimony*. Washington DC: American Psychological Association.

Ceci, S.J. (1992). Personal communication. March 13, 1992.

Ceci, S.J. and Bronfenbrenner, U. (1985). Don't forget to take the cupcakes out of the oven: Prospective memory, strategic time-monitoring, and context. *Child Development*, 56, 152-164.

Ceci, S.J. and Bruck, M. (1995). *Jeopardy in the Courtroom: A Scientific Analysis of Children's Testimony*. Washington DC: American Psychological Association.

Ceci, S.J., DeSimone, M., Putnick, M.B., Lee, J.M. and Toglia, M.P. (1990). *The role of motives in children's reports*. Paper presented at the meeting of the American Psychology-Law Society, Williamsburg, VA.

Ceci, S.J., Ross, D.F., and Toglia, M.P. (1987a). Age differences in suggestibility: Narrowing the uncertainties. In S.J. Ceci, M.P. Toglia and D.F. Ross (Eds.), *Children's Eyewitness Memory*. New York: Springer-Verlag.

Ceci, S.J., Ross, D.F., and Toglia, M.P. (1987b). Suggestibility of children's memory: Psycholegal implications. *Journal of Experimental Psychology*, 16, 38-49.

Ceci, S.J., Toglia, M.P., and Ross, D.F. (1990). The suggestibility of preschoolers' recollections: Historical perspectives on current problems. In R. Fivush and J. Hudson (Eds.), *Knowing and Remembering in Young Children*. New York: Cambridge University Press.

Chi, M.T.H. (1978). Knowledge structures and memory development. In R.S. Siegler (Ed.), *Children's Thinking: What Develops?* Hillsdale, NJ: Erlbaum.

Clarke-Stewart, A., Thompson, W.C., and Lepore, S. (1989). *Manipulating children's interpretations through interrogation*. Paper presented at the 1989 Society for Research in Child Development meetings, Kansas City, MO.

Cohen, R.L. and Harnick, M.A. (1980). The susceptibility of child witnesses to suggestion. *Law and Human Behavior*, 4, 201-210.

Cole, C.B. and Loftus, E.F. (1987). The memory of children. In S.J. Ceci, M.P. Toglia, and D.F. Ross (Eds.), *Children's Eyewitness Memory*. New York: Springer-Verlag.

Collins, G.B. and Bond, E.C. (1953). Youth as a bar to testimonial competence. *Arkansas Law Review*, 8, 100-107.

The Commission on Peace Officer Standards and Training. (1986). *Guidelines for the investigation of child physical abuse and neglect, child sexual abuse and exploitation*. Sacramento, CA: State of California.

Coon, D. (1980). *Introduction to Psychology: Exploration and Application*. New York: West Publishing Company.

Damon, W. (1988). *The Moral Child: Nurturing Children's Natural Moral Growth*. New York: The Free Press.

Davies, G., Flin, R. and Baxter, J. (1986). The child witness. *The Howard Journal*, 25, 2, 81-98.

Dent, H.R. (1982). The effects of interviewing strategies on the results of interviews with child witnesses. In A. Trankell (Ed.), *Reconstructing the Past: The Role of Psychologists in Criminal Trials*. Stockholm, PA: Norstedt & Söners Förlag.

Dent, H.R. and Stephenson, J.M. (1979). An experimental study of the effectiveness of different techniques of questioning child witnesses. *British Journal of Social and Clinical Psychology*, 13, 41-51.

DeYoung, M. (1986). A conceptual model for judging the truthfulness of a young child's allegation of sexual abuse. *American Journal of Orthopsychiatry*, 56, 550-559.

Dodd, D.H. and Bradshaw, J.M. (1980). Leading questions and memory. *Journal of Verbal Learning and Verbal Behavior*, 21, 695-704.

Dunbar, A.M. and Taylor, B.W. (1982). Children's perceptions of elementary teachers as authority figures. *Journal of Social Psychology*, 118, 249-255.

Duncan, E.M., Whitney, P., and Kunen, S. (1982). Integration of visual and verbal information in children's memories. *Child Development*, 53, 1215-1223.

Dupré, E. (1910). Le témoignage: étude psychologiique et médico-legale. *Revue Des Deux Mondes*, 55, 343-370.

Eckman, B.K. (1977). Stanley Milgram's 'obedience' studies. *Et Cetera*, March 1977.

Eysenck, H.J. and Eysenck, S.B.G. (1975). *Manual of the Eysenck Personality Questionnaire*. London: Hodder & Stoughton.

Faller, K.C. (1984). Is the child victim of sexual abuse telling the truth? *Child Abuse and Neglect*, 8, 471-481.

Finkelhor, D., Williams, L.M., and Burns, N. (1988). *Nursery Crimes: Sexual Abuse in Day Care*. Beverly Hills, CA: Sage Publications.

Fore, S. (1978). *The good-times book*. Unpublished fifth-grade yearbook. Burkburnett, Texas: Southside Elementary School.

Geffner, R. and Gross, M. (1984). Sex-role behavior and obedience to authority: A field study. *Sex Roles*, 10, 973-985.

Geis, G. and Bunn, I. (1991). And a child shall mislead them: Notes on witchcraft and child abuse accusations. In R.J. Kelly and D.E.J. MacNamara (Eds.), *Perspectives on Deviance: Dominance, Degradation, and Denigration*. Cincinnati: Anderson.

Ginsburg, H. and Opper, S. (1969). *Piaget's Theory of Intellectual Development: An Introduction*. Englewood Cliifs, NJ: Prentice-Hall.

Glennon, B. and Weisz, J.R. (1978). An observational approach to the assessment of anxiety in young children. *Journal of Consulting and Clinical Psychology*, 46, 1246-1257.

Goldsmith, S. (1988). Editor's Note. *Prosecutor's Perspective*, Volume II, Issue 1.

Goodman, G.S. (1984a). Children's testimony in historical perspective. *Journal of Social Issues*, 40, 9-32.

Goodman, G.S. (1984b). The child witness: Conclusions and future directions for research and legal practice. *Journal of Social Issues*, 40, 157-176.

Goodman, G.S. (1984c). The child witness: An introduction. *Journal of Social Issues*, 40, 1-7.

Goodman, G.S. (1991). Commentary: On stress and accuracy in research on children's testimony. In J. Doris (Ed.), *The Suggestibility of Children's Recollections: Implications for Eyewitness Testimony*. Washington DC: American Psychological Association.

Goodman, G.S. and Aman, C. (1990). Children's use of anatomically detailed dolls to recount an event. *Child Development*, 61, 1859-1871.

Goodman, G.S., Aman, C., and Hirschman, J. (1987). Child sexual and physical abuse: Children's testimony. In S.J. Ceci, M.P. Toglia, and D.F. Ross (Eds.), *Children's Eyewitness Memory*. New York: Springer-Verlag.

Goodman, G.S, Bottoms, B.L., Schwartz-Kenney, B.M., and Rudy, L. (1991). Children's testimony about a stressful event: Improving children's reports. *Journal of Narrative and Life History*, 1, 69-99.

Goodman, G.S. and Clarke-Stewart, A. (1991). Suggestibility in children's testimony: Implications for sexual abuse investigations. In J. Doris (Ed.), *The Suggestibility of Children's Recollections: Implications for Eyewitness Testimony*. Washington DC: American Psychological Association.

Goodman, G.S., Golding, J.M., and Haith, M.M. (1984). Jurors' reactions to child witnesses. *Journal of Social Issues*, 40, 139-156.

Goodman, G.S., Hepps, D., and Reed, R.S. (1986). The child victim's testimony. In A. Haralambie (Ed.), *New Issues for Child Advocates*. Phoenix, AZ: Arizona Association for Council of Children.

Goodman, G.S, Hirschman, J.E., Hepps, D., and Rudy, L. (1991). Children's memory for stressful events. *Merrill-Palmer Quarterly*, 37, 109-158.

Goodman, G.S., Hirschman, J., and Rudy, L. (1987). *Children's testimony: Research and policy implications*. Paper presented at the 1987 Society for Research in Child Development meetings, Baltimore, MD.

Goodman, G.S. and Reed, R.S. (1986). Age differences in eyewitness testimony. *Law and Human Behavior*, 10, 317-332.

Goodman, G.S., Rudy, L., Bottoms, B.L., and Aman, C. (1990). Children's concerns and memory: Issues of ecological validity in the study of children's eyewitness memory. In R. Fivush and J. Hudson (Eds.), *Knowing and Remembering in Young Children*. New York: Cambridge University Press.

Goodman, G.S. and Schwartz-Kenney, B.M. (1992). Why knowing a child's age is not enough: Influences of cognitive, social, and emotional factors on children's testimony. In R. Flin and H. Dent (Eds.), *Children as Witnesses*. London: Wiley.

Goodman, G.S., Wilson, M.E., Hazan, C., and Reed, R.S. (1989). *Children's testimony nearly four years after an event*. Paper presented at the meeting of the Eastern Psychological Association. Boston, MA.

Graham, M.H. (1985). *Witness Intimidation: The Law's Response*. Westport, CT: Quorum Books.

Gross, H. (1910). Zur Frage der Zeugenaussage. *II. Gross' Archiv*, 36, 372-382.

Heindl, R. (1909). Dei Zuverlässigkeit von Signalamentaussagen. *H. Gross' Archiv*, 33, 109-132.

Hepps, D.L. (1985). *Children's eyewitness testimony: Effects of trauma on children's memories*. Unpublished manuscript, University of Denver, Colorado.

Hofling, C.K., Brotzman, E., Dalrymple, S., Graves, N., and Pierce, C.M. (1966) An experimental study in nurse-physician relationships. *Journal of Nervous and Mental Disease*, 143, 171-180.

Hoving, K.L., Hamm, J., and Galvin, P. (1969). Social influence as a function of stimulus ambiguity at three age levels. *Developmental Psychology*, 1, 631-636.

Jackson, S. (1982). *Childhood and Sexuality*. Oxford: Basil Blackwell.

Johnson, M.K. and Foley, M.A. (1984). Differentiating fact from fantasy: The reliability of children's memory. *Journal of Social Issues*, 40, 33-50.

Johnson, M.K. and Raye, C.L. (1981). Reality Monitoring. *Psychological Review*, 88, 67-85.

Kelman, H.C. and Hamilton, V.L. (1989). *Crimes of Obedience: Toward a Social Psychology of Authority and Responsibility*. New Haven, CT: Yale University Press.

Kiesler, C.A. and Kiesler, S.B. (1969). *Conformity*. Reading, MA: Addison-Wesley.

Kilham, W. and Mann, L. (1974). Level of destructive obedience as a function of transmitter and executant roles in the Milgram obedience paradigm. *Journal of Personality and Social Psychology*, 29, 696-702.

King, M.A. (1984). *An investigation of the eyewitness abilities of children*. Unpublished doctoral thesis, University of British Columbia, Vancouver, Canada.

King, M.A. and Yuille, J.C. (1987). Suggestibility and the child witness. In S.J. Ceci, M.P. Toglia, and D.F. Ross (Eds.), *Children's Eyewitness Memory*. New York: Springer-Verlag.

Kohlberg, L. (1969). Stage and sequence: The cognitive-developmental approach to socialization. In D.A. Goslin (Ed.), *Handbook of Socialization Theory and Research*. Chicago: Rand McNally.

Kohlberg, L. (1981). *The Philosophy of Moral Development: Moral Stages and the Idea of Justice*. San Francisco: Harper & Row.

Kohlberg, L. (1984). *The Psychology of Moral Development: The Nature and Validity of Moral Stages*. San Francisco: Harper & Row.

Kwock, M.S. and Winer, G.A. (1986). Overcoming leading questions: Effects of psychosocial task variables. *Journal of Educational Psychology*, 78, 289-293.

Laupa, M. and Turiel, E. (1986). Children's conceptions of adult and peer authority. *Child Development*, 57, 405-412.

Leichtman, M.D. and Ceci, S.J. (1995). The effects of stereotypes and suggestions on preschoolers' reports. *Developmental Psychology*, 31, 568-578.

Leippe, M.R., Romanczyk, A., and Manion, A.P. (1991). Eyewitness memory for touching experiences: Accuracy and communication style differences between child and adult witnesses. *Journal of Applied Psychology*, 76, 367-379.

Lepore, S.J. (1990). Child Witness: Cognitive and social factors related to memory and testimony. *Issues in Child Abuse Accusations*, 3, 65-89

Lindberg, M. (1980). Is knowledge base development a necessary and sufficient condition for memory development? *Journal of Experimental Child Psychology*, 30, 401-410.

Lindberg, M. (1991). An interactive approach to assessing the suggestibility and testimony of eyewitnesses. In J. Doris (Ed.), *The Suggestibility of Children's Recollections: Implications for Eyewitness Testimony.* Washington DC: American Psychological Association.

Lindsay, S. and Johnson, M. (1987). Reality monitoring and suggestibility: Children's ability to discriminate among memories from different sources. In S.J. Ceci, M.P. Toglia, and D.F. Ross (Eds.), *Children's Eyewitness Memory.* New York: Springer-Verlag.

Loftus, E.F. (1977). Shifting human color memory. *Memory & Cognition*, 5, 696-699.

Loftus, E.F. (1979). *Eyewitness Testimony.* Cambridge, MA: Harvard University Press.

Loftus, E.F., Altman, D., and Geballe, R. (1975). Effects of questioning upon a witness' later recollections. *Journal of Police Science and Administration*, 3, 162-165.

Loftus, E.F. and Davies, G.M. (1984). Distortions in the memory of children. *Journal of Social Issues*, 40, 51-68.

Loftus, E.F., Miller, D.G., and Burns, J.J. (1978). Semantic integration of verbal information into visual memory. *Journal of Experimental Psychology: Human Learning and Memory.* 4, 19-31.

Loftus, E.F. and Palmer, J.C. (1974). Reconstruction of automobile destruction: An example of the interaction between language and memory. *Journal of Verbal Learning and Verbal Behavior*, 13, 585-589.

Loftus, E.F. and Zanni, G. (1975). Eyewitness testimony: The influence of the wording of a question. *Bulletin of the Psychonomic Society*, 5, 86-88.

Los Angeles Times, April 21, 1984. "McMartin lawyers key on children." Page 1.

Los Angeles Times, January 25, 1985. "McMartin student appears to recant earlier testimony." Page 1.

Los Angeles Times, January 18, 1986. "D.A. won't try 5 in McMartin case." Part 1, page 1.

Los Angeles Times, January 27, 1986. "McMartin flaw: Gaps in evidence." Part 1, page 1.

Los Angeles Times, July 28, 1990. "Reiner decided earlier against a third trial." Part 1, page 31.

Manshel, L. (1990). *Nap Time.* New York: William Morrow and Company, Inc.

Mantell, D.M. (1971). The potential for violence in Germany. *Journal of Social Issues*, 27, 101-112.

Marin, B.V., Holmes, D.L., Guth, M., and Kovac, P. (1979). The potential of children as eyewitness. *Law and Human Behavior*, 3, 295-306.

Martin, J., Lobb, B., Chapman, G.C., and Spillane, R. (1976). Obedience under conditions demanding self-immolation. *Human Relations*, 29, 4, 345-356.

McCloskey, M. and Zaragoza, M. (1985). Misleading post-event information and memory for events: Arguments and evidence against memory impairment hypotheses. *Journal of Experimental Psychology: General*, 114, 1, 1-16.

Melton, G.B. (1981). Children's Competence to testify. *Law and Human Behavior*, 5, 73-85.

Meyer, J. (1991). *Sticking to the facts? Obedience to authority in children*. Paper presented at the 1991 annual meetings of the Pacific Sociological Association, Irvine, California.

Meyer, J.F. and Geis, G. (1994). Social psychological research on child witnesses in abuse cases: Perfect answers to mostly wrong questions. *Child and Adolescent Social Work Journal*, 11, 209-220.

Milgram, S. (1963). Behavioral study of obedience. *Journal of Abnormal and Social Psychology*, 67, 371-378.

Milgram, S. (1965). Some conditions of obedience and disobedience to authority. *Human Relations*, 18, 57-75.

Milgram, S. (1972). Interpreting obedience: Error and evidence. In A.G. Miller (Ed.), *The Social Psychology of Psychological Research*. New York: The Free Press.

Milgram, S. (1973). The perils of obedience. *Harper's Magazine*. December, 282-291.

Milgram, S. (1974). *Obedience to Authority*. New York: Harper & Row.

Montessano, D.F. and Bagat, M.P. (1988). Normes et valeurs: Le concept d'obéissance chez l'enfant. *Archives de Psychologie*, 56, 23-39.

Morison, P., and Gardner, H. (1978). Dragons and dinosaurs: The child's capacity to differentiate fantasy from reality. *Child Development*, 49, 642-648.

Myers, J.E.B. (1987). The child witness: Techniques for direct examination, cross-examination, and impeachment. *Pacific Law Review*, 18, 801-942.

Neisser, U. (1979). The control of information pickup in selective looking. In A.D. Pick (Ed.), *Perception and Its Development: A Tribute to Eleanor J. Gibson*. Hillsdale, NJ: Lawrence Erlbaum Associates.

Newman, B.M. and Newman, P.R. (1984). *Development Through Life: A Psychosocial Approach*. Homewood, Illinois: The Dorsey Press.

Nissani, M. (1989a). An experimental paradigm for the study of conceptual conservationism and change. *Psychological Reports*, 65, 19-24.

Nissani, M. (1989b). Conceptual shift: A lesson on the nature of scientific discoveries. *Journal of College Science Teaching*, 19, 105-107.

Nissani, M. (1990). A cognitive reinterpretation of Stanley Milgram's observation on obedience to authority. *American Psychologist*, December, 1384-1385.

Nissani, M. and Hoefler, D.M. (in press). When theory fails. *Australian Journal of Psychology*.

Nissani, M. and Maier, C. (1990). *Further explorations of conceptual conservationism: Reconciling incompatible beliefs and observations concerning the circumference of the ellipse*. Unpublished manuscript.

Ochsner, J.E. and Zaragoza, M.S. (1988). *The accuracy and suggestibility of children's memory for neutral and criminal eyewitness events.* Paper presented at the American Psychology and Law Association Meetings, Miami, FL.

Orange County Register. January 19, 1990. "Mistakes marred case from the start, jurors say." Page A12.

Orne, M.T. and Evans, F.J. (1965). Social control in the psychological experiment: Antisocial behavior an hypnosis. *Journal of Personality and Social Psychology,* 1, 189-200.

Orne, M.T. and Holland, C.C. (1968). On the ecological validity of laboratory deceptions. *International Journal of Psychiatry,* 6, 282-293.

Ornstein, P.A., Gordon, B.N., and Larus, D.M. (1992). Children's memory for a personally experienced event: Implications for testimony. *Applied Cognitive Psychology,* 6, 49-60.

Palmer, E.L. (1966). *How elementary school children resolve experimentally produced conflicts in thinking.* Cooperative Research Project No. 3216, Department of Educational Research and Testing, Florida State University.

Parker, J.F., Haverfield, E., and Baker-Thomas, S. (1986). Eyewitness testimony of children. *Journal of Applied Social Psychology,* 16, 287-302.

Pear, T.H. and Wyatt, S. (1914). The testimony of normal and mentally defective children. *British Journal of Psychology,* 6, 388-419.

Penner, L.A., Hawkins, H.L., Dertke, M.C., Spector, P., and Stone, A. (1973). Obedience as a function of experimenter competence. *Memory & Cognition,* 1, 241-245.

Peters, D. (1987). The impact of naturally occurring stress on children's memory. In S.J. Ceci, M.P. Toglia, and D.F. Ross (Eds.), *Children's Eyewitness Memory.* New York: Springer-Verlag.

Peters, D. (1991a). The influence of stress and arousal on the child witness. In J. Doris (Ed.), *The Suggestibility of Children's Recollections: Implications for Eyewitness Testimony.* Washington DC: American Psychological Association.

Peters, D. (1991b). Commentary: Response to Goodman. In J. Doris (Ed.), *The Suggestibility of Children's Recollections: Implications for Eyewitness Testimony.* Washington DC: American Psychological Association.

Peterson, G.W. and Peters, D.F. (1985). The socialization values of low-income Appalachian white and rural black mothers: A comparative study. *Journal of Comparative Family Studies,* XVI, 75-91.

Piaget, J. (1962). *Play, Dreams, and Imitation in Childhood.* New York: W.W. Norton.

Piaget, J. (1977). *The Moral Judgement of the Child.* (Translated by Marjorie Gabain and reprinted from *The Moral Judgement of the Child,* 1932). New York: Penguin Books.

Price, D.W.W. (1984). *The development of children's comprehension of recurring episodes.* Unpublished doctoral dissertation, University of Denver, CO.

Raskin, D.C. and Yuille, J.C. (1989). Problems in evaluating interviews of children in sexual abuse cases. In S.J. Ceci, D.F. Ross and M.P. Toglia (Eds.), *Perspectives on Children's Testimony.* New York: Springer-Verlag.

Ratner, H.H., Smith, B.S., and Dion, S.A. (1986). Development of memory for events. *Journal of Experimental Child Psychology*, 41, 411-428.

Raviv, A., Bar-Tal, D., Raviv, A., and Houminer, D. (1990). Development in children's perceptions of epistemic authorities. *British Journal of Developmental Psychology*, 8, 157-169.

Ray, J.J. and Jones, J.M. (1983). Attitude to authority and authoritarianism amoung school children. *Journal of Social Psychology*, 119, 199-203.

Reinfeld, F. (1945). *Win at Chess*. New York: Dover.

Rigby, K. (1987). 'Faking good' with self-reported pro-authority attitudes and behaviours among schoolchildren. *Personality and Individual Differences*, 8, 445-447.

Rigby, K. and Schofield, P. (1985). *A children's attitude to authority scale*. School of Social Studies, Southern Australia Institute of Technology, Adelaide, South Australia.

Rosenbaum, M. (1983). Compliance. In M. Rosenbaum (Ed.), *Compliant Behavior: Beyond Obedience to Authority*. New York: Human Sciences Press.

Rudy, L. and Goodman, G.S. (1991). Effects of participation on children's reports: Implications for children's testimony. *Developmental Psychology*, 27, 527-538.

Sabini, J.P. and Silver, M. (1983). Dispositional versus situational interpretations of Milgram's obedience experiments: "The fundamental attribution error." *Journal of the Theory of Social Behavior*, 13, 147-154.

Sagatun, I. and Edwards, L. (1988). *The child as witness in the criminal courts*. Paper presented at the annual meetings of the Western Criminology Association, Monterey, California.

Saywitz, K.J. (1985). *Children's testimony: Age-related patterns of memory errors*. Paper presented at the annual meetings of the American Psychological Association.

Saywitz, K.J. (1987). Children's testimony: Age-related patterns of memory errors. In S.J. Ceci, M.P. Toglia, and D.F. Ross (Eds.), *Children's Eyewitness Memory*. New York: Springer-Verlag.

Saywitz, K.J, Goodman, G.S., and Myers, J.E.B. (1990). Can children provide accurate eyewitness reports? *Violence Update*, 1, 1-2,9-10.

Saywitz, K.J., Goodman, G.S., Nicholas, E., and Moan, S.F. (1991). Children's memories of a physical examination involving genital touch: Implications for reports of child sexual abuse. *Journal of Consulting and Clinical Psychology*, 59, 682-691.

Shanab, M.E. and Yahya, K.A. (1977). A behavioral study of obedience in children. *Journal of Personality and Social Psychology*, 35, 530-536.

Shanab, M.E. and Yahya, K.A. (1978). A cross-cultural study of obedience. *Bulletin of the Psychonomic Society*, 11, 267-269.

Stafford, C.F. (1962). The child as witness. *Washington Law Review*, 37, 303-324.

Starkey, M.S. (1949). *The Devil in Massachusetts: A Modern Inquiry into the Salem Witch Trials*. Reprinted as a Time Reading Program Special Edition, 1963. New York: Time Incorporated.

Stern, L.W. (1902). *Zur Psychologie der Aussage.* Berlin: J. Guttentag.
Stern, L.W. (1907-1908). Literatur zur Psycho. d. Aussage. *Zeits. f. angw. Psych.,* I, 429-450.
Stouthamer-Loeber, M. (1986). Lying as a problem behavior in children: a review. *Clinical Psychology Review,* 6, 267-289.
Stouthamer-Loeber, M., Postell, L.E., and Loeber, R. (1985). *Lying and verbal misinterpretation of reality in four-year-olds.* Unpublished manuscript.
Thomas, R.V. (1956). The problem of the child witness. *Wyoming Law Journal,* 10, 214-222.
Thompson, W.C., Clarke-Stewart, A., Meyer, J., Pathak, M.K., and Lepore, S. (1991). *Children's susceptibility to suggestive interrogation.* Paper presented at the annual meetings of the American Psychological Association, San Francisco, CA.
Tisak, M.S. (1986). Children's conceptions of parental authority. *Child Development,* 57, 166-176.
Toglia, M.P., Ceci, S.J., and Ross, D.F. (1987). *Bridging the gap between research and policy: How suggestible is children's memory?* Paper presented at the 1987 Society for Research in Child Development meetings, Baltimore, MD.
Toglia, M.P., Ross, D.F., Ceci, S.J., and Hembrooke, H. (1992). The suggestibility of children's memory: A social-psychological and cognitive interpretation. In M. Howe, C. Brainerd, and V. Reyna (Eds.) *The Development of Long-Term Retention.* New York: Springer-Verlag.
Toner, I.J. (1986). Punitive and nonpunitive discipline and subsequent rule-following in young children. *Child Care Quarterly,* 15, 27-37.
Uematsu, T. (1982). Reliability of eyewitness testimony, some results of experimental studies and their practical applications. In A. Trankell (Ed.), *Reconstructing the Past: The Role of Psychologists in Criminal Trials.* Stockholm, PA: Norstedt & Söners förlag.
Vandermass, M. (1991). *Does anxiety affect children's event reports?* Paper presented at the biennial meeting of the Society for Research in Child Development, Seattle, WA.
Varendonck, J. (1911). Les te'moignages d'enfants dans un proce's retentissant. Archives de Psychologie, 11, 129-171. Translated in part by C. Hazan, R. Hazan, and G. Goodman, as an appendix to G. Goodman (1984a) Children's testimony in historical perspective. *Journal of Social Issues,* 4, 9-32.
Vos, H.B.L. (1911). *Beiträge zur Psychologie der Aussage bei Schulkindern. Analyse d. Aussage über eine gehörte Erzählung.* Amersterdam: dissertation. Eigenbericht in *Zsch. f. angew. Psychol.,* 4, 375-378.
Weber, M. (1947). *The Theory of Social and Economic Organization.* (Edited by T. Parsons and translated by A.M. Henderson and T. Parsons). New York: The Free Press.
Whipple, G.M. (1909). The observer as reporter: A survey of the psychology of testimony. *Psychological Bulletin,* 6, 153-170.
Whipple, G.M. (1911). The psychology of testimony. *Psychological Bulletin,* 8, 307-309.

Whipple, G.M. (1912). Psychology of testimony and report. *Psychological Bulletin*, 9, 264-269.

Whipple, G.M. (1918). The obtaining of information: Psychology of observation and report. *Psychological Bulletin*, 15, 217-248.

White, S., Strom, G.A., Santilli, G., and Halpin, B.M. (1986). Interviewing young sexual abuse victims with anatomically correct dolls. *Child Abuse and Neglect*, 10, 519-529.

Young, W. M. (1988). *Vermont Sexual Abuse/Assault Protocol*. Reproduced as Appendix A in A.C. Salter *Treating Child Sex Offenders and Victims: A Practical Guide*. Beverly Hills, CA: Sage Publications.

Yuille, J.C. (1980). A critical examination of the psychological and practical implications of eyewitness research. *Law and Human Behavior*, 4, 335-345.

Yuille, J.C. (1988). The systematic assessment of children's testimony. *Canadian Psychology*, 29, 247-262.

Yuille, J.C. and King, M.A. (1985). *Children as witnesses*. Paper presented at the annual meetings of the American Psychological Association, Los Angeles, CA.

Zaragoza, M.S. (1987). Memory, suggestibility, and eyewitness testimony in children and adults. In S.J. Ceci, M.P. Toglia, and D.F. Ross (Eds.), *Children's Eyewitness Memory*. New York: Springer-Verlag.

Zaragoza, M.S. (1991). Preschool children's susceptibility to memory impairment. In J. Doris (Ed.), *The Suggestibility of Children's Recollections: Implications for Eyewitness Testimony*. Washington DC: American Psychological Association.

Index

Order Your Own Copy of
This Important Book for Your Personal Library!

INACCURACIES IN CHILDREN'S TESTIMONY
Memory, Suggestibility, or Obedience to Authority?

_____ in hardbound at $39.95 (ISBN: 0-7890-0167-5)

_____ in softbound at $14.95 (ISBN: 0-7890-0237-X)

COST OF BOOKS_____

OUTSIDE USA/CANADA/
MEXICO: ADD 20%_____

POSTAGE & HANDLING_____
(US: $3.00 for first book & $1.25
for each additional book)
Outside US: $4.75 for first book
& $1.75 for each additional book)

SUBTOTAL_____

IN CANADA: ADD 7% GST_____

STATE TAX_____
(NY, OH & MN residents, please
add appropriate local sales tax)

FINAL TOTAL_____
(If paying in Canadian funds,
convert using the current
exchange rate. UNESCO
coupons welcome.)

☐ **BILL ME LATER:** ($5 service charge will be added)
(Bill-me option is good on US/Canada/Mexico orders only;
not good to jobbers, wholesalers, or subscription agencies.)

☐ Check here if billing address is different from
shipping address and attach purchase order and
billing address information.

Signature_____

☐ **PAYMENT ENCLOSED: $**_____

☐ **PLEASE CHARGE TO MY CREDIT CARD.**

☐ Visa ☐ MasterCard ☐ AmEx ☐ Discover
☐ Diner's Club

Account #_____

Exp. Date_____

Signature_____

Prices in US dollars and subject to change without notice.

NAME_____

INSTITUTION_____

ADDRESS_____

CITY_____

STATE/ZIP_____

COUNTRY_____ COUNTY (NY residents only)_____

TEL_____ FAX_____

E-MAIL_____
May we use your e-mail address for confirmations and other types of information? ☐ Yes ☐ No

Order From Your Local Bookstore or Directly From
The Haworth Press, Inc.
10 Alice Street, Binghamton, New York 13904-1580 • USA
TELEPHONE: 1-800-HAWORTH (1-800-429-6784) / Outside US/Canada: (607) 722-5857
FAX: 1-800-895-0582 / Outside US/Canada: (607) 772-6362
E-mail: getinfo@haworth.com
PLEASE PHOTOCOPY THIS FORM FOR YOUR PERSONAL USE.

BOF96